SHORT WALK

————PUBS 1

Leicestershire and Rutland

Charles Whynne-Hammond

COUNTRYSIDE BOOKS
NEWBURY, BERKSHIRE

Countryside Books
3 Catherine Road
Newbury, Berkshire

ISBN 1 85306 421 1

Designed by Mon Mohan
Cover illustration by Colin Doggett
Photographs by the author
Maps by Glenys Jones

Produced through MRM Associates Ltd., Reading
Printed by J.W. Arrowsmith Ltd., Bristol

Contents

Area map showing the locations of the pub walks.

Introduction

Leicestershire is a large county, a diverse and interesting one. Its landscapes vary from the high, rugged outlines of Charnwood Forest to the flat, watery meadows of the river Wreake; from the coal-blasted, post-industrial hillscapes in the west to the unspoilt downlands in the south and wide plains in the north. Each part has its own unique character and beauty. Every corner richly repays the efforts of the walker and traveller. Rutland is altogether more intimate with its subtle contours dipping gently towards the Fens and its little pockets of woodland punctuating the hedge-fringed farmlands. To know Rutland well is to love its timeless, half-forgotten personality. In both counties the towns are still, for the most part, bustling farming communities, the villages are still quiet and old.

The walks in this book offer a range of routes across different types of terrain to reflect the great variety of countryside to be found in this part of the Midlands. Many of the routes described include shorter or longer options. These will allow readers to adapt walks to suit themselves, or else to undertake more than one walk from each starting point. There are also suggestions in the text for other walks to be planned and for other places to be visited, each pub listed acting as a focal point for numerous possible excursions.

The Ordnance Survey Maps referred to in the book form part of the Landranger series, 1:50 000 scale. All the rights of way mentioned should be walkable. Readers who find any difficulty with a public footpath should contact the local authority, which is responsible for maintaining such routes.

Generally pubs still keep 'normal' opening times – 11 am or 11.30 am to 2.30 pm, 6.30 pm or 7 pm to 11 pm. Sunday afternoon opening is now becoming common. Variations in these times are mentioned in the text. Eating times tend to be 12 noon to 1.30 pm or 2 pm and 7 pm to 10 pm. Most pubs have their own car parks and landlords will usually allow customers to leave vehicles there while going for a short walk. However, it would be polite to ask those landlords first before doing so. All the establishments in this book welcome families with children, many having special 'family rooms' and gardens with play-equipment. Nowadays, the quality and variety of food on offer in pubs is exceptional, and all the places listed have menus that should satisfy even the most discerning of tastes and diets. Real ales are now widely available. The food and drink items mentioned in the pub profiles are, of course, given only as examples. Regular dishes and daily specials may vary with time of year and changes in kitchen staff. The beers and ciders, too, may alter according to contractual arrangements with breweries and suppliers.

I should like to thank all those pub proprietors who supplied me with valuable information about their establishments. I am also indebted to Glenys Jones for drawing the maps and to Gwen Cassell who helped with the final draft.

Charles Whynne-Hammond
Spring 1996

Publisher's Note

We hope that you obtain considerable enjoyment from this book; great care has been taken in its preparation. However, changes of landlord and actual closures are sadly not uncommon. Likewise, although at the time of publication all routes followed public rights of way or permitted paths, diversion orders can be made and permissions withdrawn.

We cannot of course be held responsible for such diversion orders and any inaccuracies in the text which result from these or any other changes to the routes nor any damage which might result from walkers trespassing on private property. However, we are anxious that all details covering the walks and the pubs are kept up to date and would therefore welcome information from readers which would be relevant to future editions.

1 Shackerstone
The Rising Sun

Dogs allowed in conservatory

This attractive little canalside village is now the terminus for the Battlefield Steam Railway Line. Regular passenger trains run from here to the Bosworth Field battle site, 4 miles to the south.

The Rising Sun is a traditional village pub which has been extended to accommodate extra custom, incorporating what was once an adjacent barn. It is now a popular restaurant called the Tudor Barn Grill. In the carpeted and low ceilinged main bar-cum-lounge there are wood-panelled walls, adorned with intriguingly illuminated etching prints, and comfortable cushioned bench seating. There is also a poolroom with satellite television and another room set aside for families.

The real ales served include Marston's Pedigree and several guest beers, such as John Smith's Bitter and Nethergate Bitter. Red Rock and Strongbow ciders are also available, as too are various wines sold by the glass. The regular menu ranges from rolls, sandwiches and jacket potatoes to steaks, grills, chicken, fish and salad dishes. This is supplemented by home-cooked daily specials and there are always four or five vegetarian dishes available, including pasta and vegetable bakes. The Rising Sun is a friendly, welcoming place which keeps normal pub opening times.

Telephone: 01827 880215.

How to get there: Shackerstone stands in the middle of unspoilt countryside between Coalville and Hinckley, 15 miles west of Leicester. Situated between the A444 and A447 the village is easily reached from Twycross and Nailstone. You will find the pub opposite the church at the southern end of the village.

Parking: In the pub car park, or along the village street. Alternatively, use the public car park at the northern end of Shackerstone near the Steam Railway Line.

Length of the walk: 3 miles. OS map: Landranger 140 Leicester and Coventry (inn GR 375067).

The long distance footpath called The Leicestershire Round, which circumnavigates the county, passes through Shackerstone. So too does the Ashby Canal, and between them they offer good walking opportunities in the area, as well as the chance to observe the varied local wildlife. This level and easy to follow circular route incorporates the scenic canal towpath, a quiet country lane and a farmland footpath. The attractive village of Congerstone, where some pretty cottages cluster around a double road junction, is worth exploring along the way.

The Walk

Turn right outside the Rising Sun and then right again to reach the Ashby Canal. At the bridge, take the path on the left to join the towpath. A signpost informs you that Congerstone is 1½ miles away to the right. This walk along the canalside is extremely pleasant. There are narrow boats moored alongside and views extend eastwards across the meadows towards the village of Barton in the Beans. On the far side of the waterway is the Battlefield Steam Railway Line. Originally built in 1873, this 4½ mile section of track operates a regular steam service linking Shackerstone to Shenton, close to the site of the Battle of Bosworth. The Ashby Canal is somewhat older, dating back to the first decade of the 19th

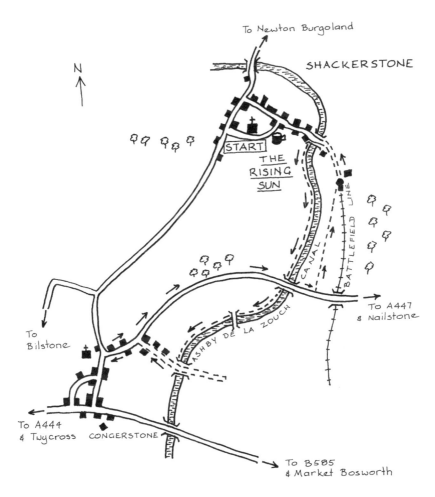

century. This was cut between Bedworth (on the Coventry Canal) and the Ashby Woulds coalfield, to link the Midlands factories with the iron ore and coal deposits of Leicestershire.

Remain on the towpath for about a mile, then at the third bridge (numbered 49 above the arch), climb the stile on your right to reach a gravel track and then descend to the road. Turn left into Congerstone and spend an enjoyable half-hour or so looking around this charming village. Despite being heavily restored in the 19th century, St Mary's Church is most attractive, and its peaceful churchyard is the perfect place in which to rest awhile.

The return journey begins along Barton Road, retracing your steps along the lane used when approaching the village. Instead of returning to the canal, continue along the road for about a mile, as it bears right and passes a small woodland. There is little traffic and the route is very quiet. In due course, cross the bridge over the Ashby Canal, then in about 100 yards take the waymarked footpath on your left (arrowed yellow-topped post).

The footpath is not well defined, but the route is obvious. Head straight across the large field, keeping the canal parallel to your left, towards the distant, red-brick building (the old station house). Immediately beyond is the Battlefield Steam Railway Line complex, complete with Victorian tearooms, various railway relics and, down by the canal, a small picnic site. To reach the Railway and Museum, cross the stile at the far end of the footpath. To return to the Rising Sun, continue down the gravel track and turn left just after the canal bridge.

Places of interest nearby

At Coalville (6 miles north-east) is the *Snibston Discovery Park* which features a science and industry museum and a colliery exhibition. Close to the Discovery Park is the *Swannington Heritage Trail* with its railway incline and various industrial archaeological displays. Near Ashby-de-la-Zouch (7 miles north) is the *Moira Furnace and Craft Workshops* centre, a well preserved blast furnace with accompanying museum displays. South of the above is the *Measham Museum* of village life.

2 Market Bosworth
Ye Olde Red Lion Hotel

11-12 pM
2.15 - 18.30 pM
Dogs allowed
when not
serving food

This attractive little market town is famous for its association with the final battle in the Wars of the Roses. In 1485, on a field just 2 miles away, Richard III was killed, so leaving the throne free for Henry VII, the first of the Tudor monarchs. Ye Olde Red Lion probably dates from about that time, although later alterations have modified its original appearance. Inside there are beams, an attractive brick chimney breast and numerous oak posts. The decor is traditional, with plate shelves, brassware and old prints hung on the plain walls. There is one large main bar, which contains several sections which are semi-separate. To the rear of the hotel is a covered patio where families tend to gather.

It is well known for the range of real ales on offer – and deservedly so. The blackboard list may feature Banks's, Theakston, Camerons and other guest beers. Draught Scrumpy Jack and Strongbow ciders, several stouts and various wines are also served. The choice of food is equally impressive, from traditional bar snacks, such as rolls, burgers and items with chips, to main meals

11

and specials like lasagne, grills, meat pies and seafood dishes. On Sundays, the roast lunches are especially popular. This is a very pleasant, friendly establishment keeping normal pub opening times. Telephone: 01455 291713.

How to get there: Market Bosworth is situated on the B585, just to the west of the A447 Ibstock to Hinckley road, 6 miles north of Hinckley. The Red Lion will be found close to the centre of town, on the corner of the road leading north to Carlton.

Parking: There is a pub car park. Parking elsewhere in Market Bosworth may be difficult, although vehicles can be left at the roadside, along the lane to Carlton.

Length of the walk: 4 miles. OS map: Landranger 140 Leicester and Coventry (inn GR 407032).

This is a long, but very easy, circular walk incorporating the village of Sutton Cheney, which is reached via a gated and generally traffic-free metalled road. The return follows clear, well waymarked footpaths across open farmland. There are a few stiles to climb but these should not cause any problems. The countryside around Market Bosworth is extremely pretty and there are fine views to be enjoyed. The area immediately south of the town is called Bosworth Park and shows clear signs of having been landscaped, with lakes, copses and tree-lined vistas indicating 18th century estate planning. This is also hunting country and fox coverts are scattered across the hills.

The Walk
From the Red Lion walk up Main Street and then turn left along Market Place. Beyond the Old Black Horse Inn, continue straight on, ignoring both Shenton Lane on the right and Rectory Lane on the left. The route required is signposted as a gated road to Sutton Cheney. Proceed down this lane, then where the houses end, go through a gate and continue ahead. Gated roads are not well used by vehicles, so the 2 mile walk to Sutton Cheney is extremely quiet and pleasant. Over to the left is countryside that once formed part of Bosworth Park, landscaped during the 18th century. The distant

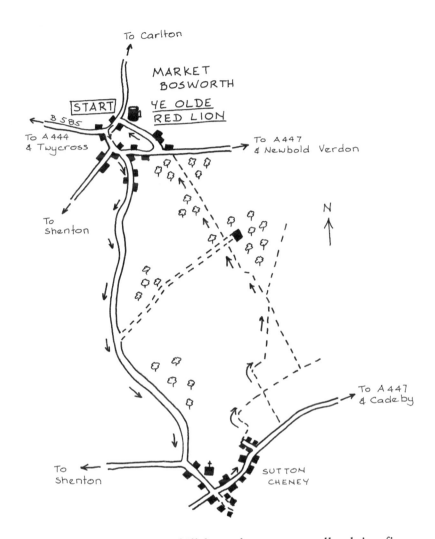

monument, standing on a hillslope close to a woodland, is a figure of Hercules. This estate was once owned by the Dixie family, which did many a philanthropic deed. The old Grammar School, situated in the Market Place, was endowed by the family, and much of the rebuilding of Market Bosworth was financed by them.

Sutton Cheney boasts a 13th-century church with Richard III associations, a farmhouse that contains part of an Elizabethan mansion, and a row of almshouses founded in 1612. Turn left at the

The market place at Market Bosworth.

junction near the church, along the road to Cadeby, and then past the attractive and old Hercules Inn, which is named after the nearby monument. The footpath back to Market Bosworth begins at the top end of the cul-de-sac called The Square, which is on the left after passing Hall Farm. Beyond the last house, a footpath signpost points the way.

The route is very clear. Go right, then left around the corner of a field, and then turn right again to cross the middle of the next field in a north-easterly direction. The path is tractor-rutted. After about 400 yards you meet another track at right-angles. Turn left to reach a yellow post bearing arrow discs. At this point, turn right to follow a field edge, keeping the hedgerow to your right. At the next corner, bear half-left to cross the following field diagonally. In due course, you come down to a junction of paths, where more arrow discs point in different directions. Continue north along a field edge, with the hedgerow now to your left. A left, then right kink takes you across a little stream and uphill beside a woodland, to reach a handsome, Edwardian-style farmhouse. The route described so far may sound complicated but, in fact, the path is very clear throughout, due to the local farmer making a good job of footpath maintenance.

The route beyond the farmhouse is even easier to follow. Climb several stiles and continue northwards. A wide grassy track winds between a succession of fields and along a line of trees. You pass a lake on the left and then a small woodland, also on your left. In due course, walk through another woodland to reach an area laid out as a park, with a network of pathways and bench seats positioned at irregular intervals. In fact, this last stretch is through a council run arboretum, in which the old Bosworth Hall grounds have been re-organised into an area for public use. Conveniences are provided and a pleasant lakeside walk has been created. To reach the Red Lion continue through this arboretum up to the road, and then along the one-way system in the opposite direction to the traffic.

Places of interest nearby

Bosworth Battlefield, incorporating a Country Park and Visitor Centre, is just 2 miles south of Market Bosworth. An exhibition and film theatre help recreate the battle events, whilst a 'Battle Trail' guides visitors around the principal sites. *Twycross Zoo*, with its special attractions for children, like train and donkey rides, lies 6 miles away to the north-west. At *Mallory Park* (3 miles east) regular motorbike races are held and at Desford (nearby) you will find a *Tropical Bird Garden*.

3 Castle Donington
The Cross Keys

Dogs allowed under control

Despite its close proximity to a motor racing circuit, an airport and a large power station, Castle Donington is actually a pleasant little town. The old centre clusters around a 13th-century church and contains a wealth of interesting buildings. Many of these are 18th century, but the timber-framed Key House in the High Street dates from 1636.

There are also several good pubs here, including the Turks Head, the Lamb and the Tudor Inn, which all serve an excellent range of food and drink and can be equally recommended. The Cross Keys, however, is different, since it is a traditional alehouse that prides itself on its wide range of real ales. Half a dozen or more of these are available at any one time – the full list being written up on the blackboard above the bar. There is Marston's Pedigree and Theakston Bitter, and such guest brews as Morland Old Speckled Hen and Wadworth 6X. Various draught ciders are also served, including Strongbow and a traditional farmhouse scrumpy, and fruit wines are included on the wine list. Not that the food quality is ignored! All is home-cooked and excellent value. From rolls, salads and ploughman's lunches to steak and kidney pie, grills and fish dishes, the choice is wide. Vegetarians are offered pasta and vegetable bakes and special requests can be made in advance.

Inside, the atmosphere is old-fashioned and cosy. The one large bar room is separated into five sections, giving the feel of different rooms. There are low ceilings, a brick fireplace with open grate, tiled floors and plain walls hung with pictures. In one corner a large model warplane hangs from the ceiling. Normal pub opening times are kept.

Telephone: 01332 812214.

How to get there: Castle Donington is located in the far north-west corner of Leicestershire, close to the Derbyshire and Nottinghamshire borders. It is only 2 miles west of the M1 (Junction 24), which is also where the A6 and A453 converge. The Cross Keys will be found on the B6540, downhill from the town centre.

Parking: The pub has a car park and free public car parks are situated close to the town centre. Vehicles may also be left in some of the side streets.

Length of the walk: 3 miles. OS map: Landranger 129 Nottingham and Loughborough (inn GR 446275).

There is a power station immediately west of Castle Donington and another 4 miles north-east, resulting in lines of pylons crossing the nearby landscape. The M1 motorway and the East Midlands Airport are also situated close by. Nevertheless, there is attractive countryside around the town and some scenic walks to be enjoyed. The circular route described here is well walked by both locals and visitors, as it takes in the pretty villages of Hemington and Lockington. The outward journey is along clear footpaths across farmland, the return route follows a long-established gravel surfaced lane. Numerous old and interesting buildings are passed, and pleasant views can be enjoyed. For a shorter circuit Lockington can be omitted.

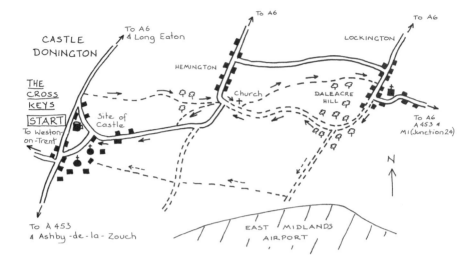

The Walk

Turn right outside the Cross Keys and walk downhill to the junction with Hillside, which comes down from the right. The Tudor Inn is opposite, over to your left. Cross over Hillside and immediately turn right along the footpath signposted. The path passes between hedges, soon to reach more open countryside, with a grassy hill rising away to your right. It was upon this hill that Donington Castle once stood. This was a Norman stronghold, built to control the crossing point of the river Trent, before being demolished in the 16th century.

The route to Hemington is not difficult to follow. The path crosses a number of fields and several stiles, all the while keeping the hill slope to the right. At the far end, it rises a little to pass through a copse and then joins a tarmac path that descends from the right. Bear left to go through a kissing-gate and meet the road at a junction. Turn left to view the main part of the village, otherwise, turn right along Church Lane to continue the circular route. You will return to this spot later. Hemington boasts many timber-framed buildings and the village should be explored at leisure. The Hall is a fine medieval building and the Nunnery dates from the 18th century. Sadly, the 13th-century church has been in ruins since Tudor times. Today, just a few ivy-clad walls hint at its former glory.

18

The path to Lockington begins alongside this ruined church. Go through a wooden pedestrian gate and continue eastwards beside a paddock fence. The route is very clear. Proceed through a kissing-gate and skirt the northern slope of Daleacre Hill. In the fields down to your left, you should notice the undulations of ridge-and-furrow, remnants of ancient strip farming systems. Beyond another kissing-gate the path leads you over the hill slope, beside a woodland and then down to Lockington. Turn right when you meet the road and walk along Main Street. At the next junction, either go straight on to continue the circuit, or turn left up Church Street, to visit the 13th-century Church of St Nicholas. The latter should not be missed. Inside, you will see some fine Gothic carving, numerous interesting tombs and, most striking of all, a magnificent tympanum above the chancel screen.

The return to Hemington follows the route of a medieval road. Today, it is a wide gravel track running between hedgerows. Beyond the houses up Main Street, go through an iron bar gate and then, 200 yards further on, turn right. If you wish to extend your walk follow the gravel track that leads uphill from this junction, then in ½ mile, at the top of the hill, turn right along a tractor-rutted footpath back to Castle Donington. The return from Hemington can be made along the tarmac path mentioned earlier. This brings you to the road at the edge of Castle Donington, where you turn right to reach the town centre.

Places of interest nearby

East Midlands Airport has an *Aeropark and Visitor Centre* with old aircraft exhibits and displays showing flight technology. At the racing circuit is the *Donington Park Collection of Racing Cars*. At *Kegworth Museum* (3 miles east) there are exhibits of Victoriana and war memorabilia, and at Long Whatton (2 miles further south) you will find *Whatton Gardens*, with its 26 acres of formal and wild plant layouts.

Dogs allowed ✓

④ Dunton Bassett
The Merrie Monk

This attractive and quiet village has no fewer than three pubs. In the centre, downhill from the church, is the Dunton Bassett Arms and, round the corner, stands the Crown and Thistle. The Merrie Monk is on the far side of the main road, a short distance away. All three can be recommended. Of the three, the Merrie Monk is, perhaps, the most typical of a villagers' pub. It is cosy and friendly, unpretentiously decorated, offers various games facilities and serves a limited range of food and drink. All the customers seem to know each other and conversation is always cheery. But strangers should not be put off, both walkers and other travellers are made extremely welcome, as are children.

There is one main bar counter serving two separate rooms, a lounge and a public bar. Although beamed, the ceilings are high (the building is not that old) and the plain walls are hung with drawings of local scenes. The bar snacks are made to order and offer excellent value for money. There are sandwiches, salads, cob rolls with various fillings, omelettes and dishes with chips. Vegetarians will be happily accommodated with specially cooked items prepared on request. Those seeking full evening meals should patronise the other pubs in the village. The Merrie Monk is a Marston's house offering Pedigree real ale, plus a guest beer like Banks's Mild. Srongbow draught cider and various wines are also served.

Normal pub opening times are kept. This is a popular pub and should not be missed.

Telephone: 01455 209117.

How to get there: Dunton Bassett lies just off the A426, 9 miles south of Leicester and 4 miles north of Lutterworth. The M1 motorway is only a mile away, the nearest exit being junction 20 at Lutterworth. The Merrie Monk will be found east of the A426, on the road to Ashby Magna.

Parking: There is a large pub car park and vehicles can also be left along the side of the lane in front. The Dunton Bassett Arms and the Crown and Thistle also have car parks.

Length of the walk: 2 miles. OS map: Landranger 140 Leicester and Coventry (inn GR 553908).

The Leicestershire Round long distance footpath passes through Dunton Bassett and a good walk can be enjoyed in each direction, to Leire in the west, and Willoughby Waterleys to the north-east of the village. Other paths can also be explored, for this is a very pleasant part of the county. This short circuit follows the Leicestershire Round to Dunton Bassett centre and then returns through the village lanes. This is an old and interesting settlement, with a host of buildings to admire, including the church which dates from the 13th century. The route is clear throughout, but some stiles must be climbed on the outward journey.

The Walk

Turn right outside the Merrie Monk and walk down the lane towards the bridge that crosses the M1 motorway. This is not a busy lane, but there is a pavement nonetheless. Shortly before the motorway turn right again. A footpath signpost points down a flight of steps and informs you that this is the Leicestershire Round and that Dunton Bassett is ½ mile away. The route is clear all the

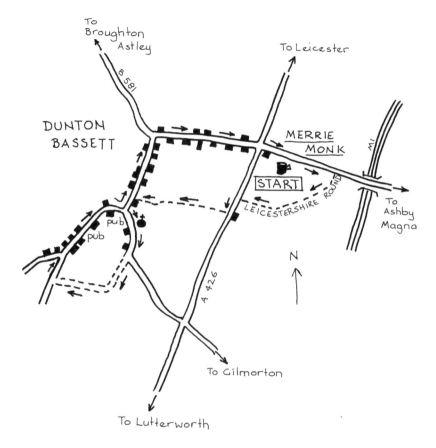

way. From the stile at the bottom of the steps cross the field diagonally half-right. In the following field, follow the hedgerow up to the A426.

Turn left, cross over and continue along the footpath on the far side. The footpath signpost will be found almost opposite the petrol filling station. Follow the edge of this next field, keeping the hedgerow to your left, until you reach the second stile (the first leading simply into a sports field). Once over the stile, continue in the same direction, now with the hedgerow to your right. A double stile then takes you across a ditch into the next field, from where you head towards the houses. In the field corner, a narrow path leads to the road. In this last field, notice the lumps and bumps in the grass and the earthy undulations. A lost medieval landscape lies beneath.

Medieval Dunton Bassett was a different shape to the modern village. The fields immediately north of the church were once covered by cottages and gardens, and the land up by the B581, now built over, were sheep pastures. This change occurred as a result of the building of the coaching road during the 18th century and construction of the railway in the 19th century. The former is now the A426, the latter has been dismantled, but once ran alongside the M1 motorway. During the 19th century the village was inhabited by framework knitters and became fairly prosperous – some of the Victorian buildings still bearing testimony to this.

The walk around Dunton Bassett is pleasant and time should be taken to look at the church, cottages and gardens. Emerging onto the road turn left, and shortly bear left again up Church Lane. Beyond the church, where the road turns sharp left, go straight on along a gravel track signposted as a bridleway. This heads south, then west, to reach the far end of the village. There you turn right to follow the village street all the way back to the Merrie Monk, passing both the other village pubs on the way.

Places of interest nearby
At Sutton in the Elms (3 miles north-west) is the *Mill on the Soar Falconry Centre*, which has flying demonstrations by various birds of prey. Just 4 miles further west is *Burbage Common*, forming part of the ancient Hinckley Forest. Here are footpaths, bird-watching hides and picnic sites. Between Burbage Common and Dunton Bassett is Sharnford and *Fosse Meadows*, which can be explored by country lovers.

No Dogs

5 Walcote
The Tavern Inn

Walcote is not a big place, and has no large Gothic church, but it is a busy place. The A427 speeds through and junction 20 of the M1 motorway is only a mile away. Yet few of the motorists that drive through Walcote see the best of the village. The oldest and most attractive cottages stand away from the main road.

The Tavern Inn, however, does stand on the A427 and, as a result, has become a very popular stopping place for travellers seeking refreshment. It deserves its popularity, for it offers a warm welcome, friendly service and an excellent range of food and drink. Children are welcome, both inside and out, and are offered their own food portions. Inside, there are high beamed ceilings, a wood surround bar counter and walls hung with past and present pictures of the village. The public bar is reached from the car park, the lounge and dining room being situated beyond, to one side. The former has a skittle table, the latter are decorated with plates and horse brasses. In short, all is very traditional and most comfortable.

The real ales served include Theakston XB and Marston's

Pedigree, the draught ciders are Scrumpy Jack and Dry Blackthorn and the wines are mostly French. The food is superb. Bar snacks range from burgers, sandwiches and salads to main meals, such as beef in ale pie, grilled trout, fisherman's pie and mixed grill. Sweets include gateaux, tarts and ice cream. Vegetarians are offered a wide choice, including vegetable curry, mushroom bake, chilli burger and vegetable tagliatelle. Indeed, all the items listed on the blackboard are temptingly mouth-watering.

Normal pub opening times are kept.

Telephone: 01455 553338.

How to get there: Walcote lies just 2 miles east of Lutterworth on the A427 Market Harborough road.

Parking: There is a pub car park. Vehicles can also be left in the village but, preferably, not along the busy A427.

Length of the walk: 3½ miles. OS map: Landranger 140 Leicester and Coventry (inn GR 567837).

Despite the proximity of the motorway, this walk explores a very pretty and unspoilt area of countryside. The route includes the quiet hamlet of Misterton, adjacent to a private landscaped estate, and crosses some of the tributary valleys that feed the river Swift. Trackways, country lanes and footpaths across farmland are all used. For the most part, the route is clear and well signposted. There are stiles to climb and a few plank bridges to cross, but nothing should prove too difficult.

The Walk

The route begins up Brook Street, which runs alongside the Tavern Inn. Those wishing to take the shorter and easier way to Misterton, should turn left up Chapel Lane and then, at its far end, continue along a tarmac path that becomes a gravel track. Those wanting a slightly longer route should walk to the top of Brook Street and turn left. A footpath will then lead you along the edge of two large fields, eventually reaching a squeeze-stile and the gravel track mentioned above, on which you turn right. The gravel track in question is, in fact, an unmetalled lane that marks the route of an old road. In medieval times, before the present stretch of main road

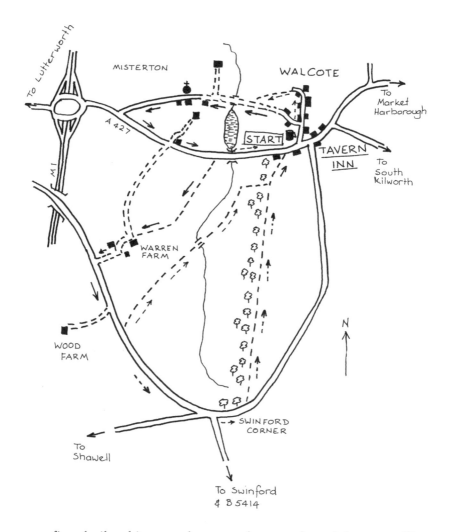

was first built, this was the way that coach and horse traffic trundled. The route was altered with the building of Misterton Hall and the coming of the turnpikes.

The hamlet of Misterton, which you approach by passing a lake, is an attractive little spot. The church dates from the 14th century, the rectory is Victorian mock-Tudor, and the yew trees cast their dark shade over the tranquil scene. It is hard to believe that the M1 motorway is only ½ mile away. The village is now much smaller

Misterton Hall lodge.

than it once was. The Black Death in the 14th century and the expansion of sheep grazing in Tudor and Stuart times caused many of its inhabitants to die or move away. In many of the fields, you can still see the grassy undulations marking the sites of medieval cottages and lanes that have long since disappeared. A mile northeast, another village totally vanished. This was Poultney, and its site is now occupied by Great Poultney Farm.

Pass Misterton church and continue west along the gravel lane, until you reach the main A427. Turn left and walk along the pavement for about ½ mile, soon to pass the lodge and entrance gateway to Misterton Hall on your left.

Those wishing to curtail their walk can return to Walcote directly along the main road. Others should cross over and take the footpath signposted on the right. This heads across the middle of a field, up and over the skyline, and then half-right alongside a hedgerow to Warren Farm. Close to a barn, you meet a farm track and follow it through the farmstead. On the far side, a tree-lined drive leads down to a road, where you turn left.

Two routes now present themselves. The longer, and easier way keeps to the road for a mile to Swinford Corner, and then turns left

27

down a footpath that follows a belt of trees all the way back to Walcote. The shorter, but less clearly marked, route uses the footpath which is signposted left, soon after the entrance to Wood Farm. It cuts diagonally across a large field, follows a stream for a short way, and then turns right along a field edge to reach the belt of trees mentioned above. From there, it crosses diagonally to reach the main road, passing beneath a line of pylons.

Places of interest nearby

Lutterworth (2 miles west) is an interesting town, with a museum, ancient church and numerous old buildings. *Stanford Hall* (3 miles south) dates from the late 17th century and contains antique furniture and some fine old paintings. The gardens are beautiful and should not be missed.

6 Arnesby
The Cock Inn

In Baptist circles Arnesby is famous for being the birthplace, in 1764, of Robert Hall the hymn writer. He was the son of a Baptist minister and lived at the old Manse, next to the chapel. The building is still used for religious meetings. The Cock Inn stands close by and, itself, is a popular place for gatherings. But the groups that come here are rather less religiously committed, and rather more gastronomically committed, than their ecclesiastical neighbours. For this pub serves an excellent range of food and drink. Parties of up to 50 can be catered for by arrangement, and, at weekends, the restaurant operates a carvery.

This is an old building and the inside has been sympathetically decorated in traditional style. The rooms are large and set around a central bar counter, with the public bar to the left, the lounge to the right and the restaurant behind. There are low ceiling beams, inglenook brick fireplaces and plain walls hung with pictures and old photos of local scenes. Spindle screens sub-divide the lounge and the furniture is wooden.

Real ales served include Tetley Bitter and Mansfield Old Baily, the draught cider is Addlestones and a full range of wines is offered. The regular menu is supplemented by daily specials and there is plenty for everyone, in both choice and portions. Bar snacks include sandwiches, baguettes and salads; main meals range from lasagne, chilli, cottage pie, curry and vegetable bake to roasts, grills and fish dishes. There is also a full sweet menu, with cakes, ices and puddings.

The Cock Inn keeps normal pub opening times, but closes on Monday lunchtimes. At weekends live entertainment is provided.

Telephone: 01533 478251.

WRONG NUMBER

How to get there: Arnesby is situated just off the A50 between Leicester to Husbands Bosworth, 8 miles from Leicester. Fleckney lies 2 miles to the east. The Cock Inn will be found at the eastern end of the village, close to the A50.

Parking: There is a large pub car park. Vehicles can also be left in the village streets, which are not busy.

Length of the walk: 4 miles. OS map: Landranger 140 Leicester and Coventry (inn GR 618925).

Considering the close proximity of Leicester, the countryside around Arnesby is surprisingly quiet and unspoilt. There are many footpaths in the area and walks can be enjoyed in all directions. The Leicestershire Round long distance footpath passes through this area, offering excellent walking both east and west. This circular walk is very easy to follow, the way being well signposted and the undulations gentle. Footpaths are followed across farmland to Peatling Magna, a charming little village with many ancient cottages. The return route follows a gated road, which is almost devoid of traffic. Those with time should also look around Arnesby itself. It boasts a church dating back to Norman times and an interesting grid pattern of lanes, which was planned in the Middle Ages.

The Walk

Outside the Cock Inn turn left, not down St Peters Road into the village centre, but along the Lutterworth Road which heads west along the northern edge of Arnesby. In about 300 yards turn right.

The windmill, complete with sails, that you see ahead is a private residence, and the drive up to it is **not** a public right of way. The waymarked footpath actually goes up beside the drive, along a field edge, and then crosses it by way of a pair of stiles. Beyond these, walk past the gardens of the Mill residence and admire the selection of statuary on the lawns. At the end of the garden fence a plank bridge and stile take you into the open countryside.

The route to Peatling Magna is easy to follow. There are yellow-topped posts marking the way and arrow discs pointing the direction. From the Mill, bear half-right and then walk diagonally across a number of fields. In due course, you will see the spire of Peatling Magna church peeping up above the distant trees, and you aim for that. The countryside all around is beautiful, the low hills affording expansive views. The first few fields you cross were once used for grazing deer, but now just sheep and horses wander about. Throughout the journey, you should also notice the ridge-and-furrow undulations in the pastures. These are some of the best examples in Leicestershire of strip farming topography.

Shortly before reaching Peatling Magna you meet a country lane. Follow this as it curves into the village. What a pleasant spot this is! Tall trees and leafy lanes commingling with a cluster of old cottages. The Old Cock Inn looks most inviting, and if open, it should certainly be explored. The village has a timeless quality, and could not have changed much since it was the birthplace of Elizabeth

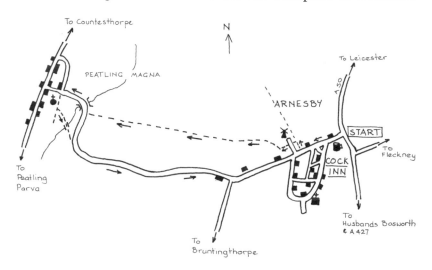

Arnesby windmill.

Jervis, who grew up to be the devoted wife of Dr. Johnson, the 18th-century writer and wit.

The return route to Arnesby begins at the bottom corner of the churchyard, where a stile leads into a field. Turn left and walk down across this hummocky field. Do **not** follow the direction of the arrow (straight on), which will take you to Bruntingthorpe. Under the trees in the far hedgerow you will find a stile and plank bridge over a stream. Bear half-right on the far side to meet the road, and follow it all the way back to Arnesby. It is a gated road and so liable to be empty of traffic. Simply enjoy the scenery, and the peace and quiet.

Places of interest nearby

At North Kilworth (5 miles south) narrow boats are hired out for day trips along the Grand Union Canal, information obtainable at *Kilworth Marina*. North, in the southern suburbs of Leicester, is the *Wigston Framework Knitters Museum*, showing an 18th-century knitters house and workshop, and the *Wigston Magna Folk Museum*, with its unique collection of farming and industrial implements.

(7) Gumley
The Bell Inn

In Saxon times, when this part of England belonged to the Kings of Mercia, Gumley was an important place. There was a royal palace here and a thriving settlement had developed at the centre of a rich farming region. Today, however, the village is quiet and unspoilt, with many old cottages stretching in a line up a hillside lane. Within this delightful scene, the Bell Inn performs well the role of traditional village inn. It is a freehouse offering a friendly welcome and a wide range of food and drink. To the left of the entrance hall is a small cosy dining room, which doubles as a family room; to the right is a large room, part acting as a public bar, part as a lounge. The decor is unfussy, featuring low beams, bare walls and wooden furniture. Outside, at the back, is a small enclosed beer garden.

The real ales served include Charles Wells Bombardier and Boddingtons Bitter, with Scrumpy Jack cider also available on draught. There is also a wide selection of wines. But it is the food offered that especially attracts the customers. A good range of light snacks and main meals is augmented on Sundays by special lunch

menus. These are written up on the blackboard. Starters might include garlic mushrooms, soups and pâtés, with main course options ranging from beef Wellington and steak and kidney pudding to salmon en croute. There is always a choice for vegetarians, which may include an excellent looking mushroom stroganoff, and the desserts are wickedly exciting. The Bell Inn keeps normal pub opening times.
Telephone: 0116 2792476.

How to get there: Gumley nestles in the attractive hill country of southern Leicestershire, 4 miles north-west of Market Harborough. It can be reached from the A6 trunk road, turning west through Foxton. Alternatively, you can drive there from Lubenham, which stands on the A427 Market Harborough to Rugby road. The Bell Inn stands at the southern end of the village.

Parking: There is a small car park in front of the Bell Inn. Vehicles can also be left along the roadside of the main village street.

Length of the walk: 3 miles (or shorter options). OS map: Landranger 141 Kettering and Corby (inn GR 684898).

Gumley is an excellent walking centre. There are footpaths, bridleways and gated roads radiating out in all directions; the scenery is superb, and the ground underfoot is generally dry. The stroll down to Foxton Locks, on the Grand Union Canal, is very popular and the towpath provides an attractive route. This walk, however, is to the pretty village of Laughton and back. The outward route is marked clearly throughout with yellow-painted signposts and blue arrow discs. There are some stiles to negotiate. The return is by gated road.

The Walk
Turn left outside the Bell Inn and walk up the main village street. After a short distance turn left along a narrow path that runs between the houses. This stands almost opposite a red telephone box and is signposted as a bridleway. Soon a gate takes you through to the open fields. Two arrow discs are nailed up; one pointing half-left, the other half-right. Follow the latter, keeping to the edge of the field, and enjoy the views ahead, across hummocky hills and

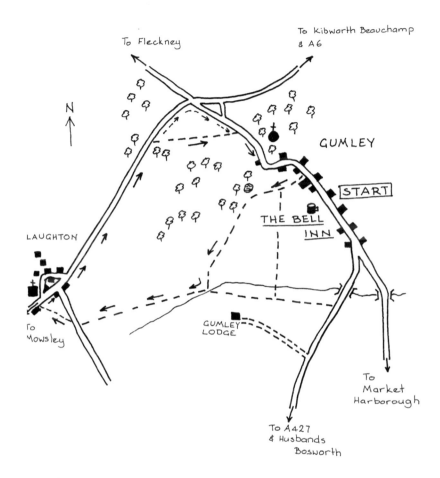

To Fleckney

To Kibworth Beauchamp & A6

N

GUMLEY

START

THE BELL INN

LAUGHTON

To Mowsley

GUMLEY LODGE

To Market Harborough

To A427 & Husbands Bosworth

into deep valleys, dotted with clumps of trees and wide hedgerows. In the far corner of the field a gate leads you through, the path running down into an attractive little combe. At the bottom you will see a small lake. Aim to the left of this.

The route is clear throughout. Follow the directions indicated by the blue arrow discs and aim for the yellow-painted posts. The bridleway runs fairly straight across a number of fields, many of which show the signs of ridge-and-furrow cultivation, the Saxon strip-field method of farming. Up from the valley bottom, near the lake, you continue towards the distant farmhouse called Gumley Lodge, a building which has seen better days.

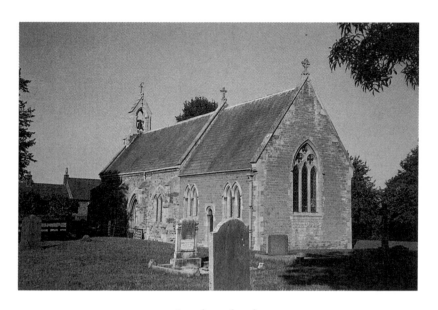

Laughton church.

Do **not** go through the last gateway before this building however. Instead, bear right and keep the little stream to your left, then at the next hedgerow, another blue arrow disc points the way forward. From here the route is almost dead straight. Soon the bridleway becomes a footpath and stiles appear, to carry you from one field to the next. But still the yellow posts and arrow discs guide you onwards. Eventually you reach a country lane. Cross straight over to another stile. From here, the footpath leads diagonally across two fields to a large barn, where you curve round to meet the road in the village of Laughton.

The shorter option here is to the right. The longer, and more interesting, option is to the left. This will lead you around the village and give you a chance to appreciate this lovely little settlement. You will find a cluster of elegant houses, old farms, an attractive church and the fascinating Killock House, which boasts a sundial on the side wall and a waterpump in the porch. The way back is simplicity itself. Just follow the lane signposted as a gated road. Gumley village is 1¼ miles away. This is a very quiet lane and offers superb views either side.

About half-way along, a cattle-grid leads you through into a more open landscape and Saddington Reservoir can be seen way across to your left. The Northamptonshire Heights can be seen to the right. Beyond a small clump of Scots pine trees a footpath leads off diagonally to the right, to cut off a corner. You may choose to follow this. However, if you keep to the road, you can walk across a cricket pitch that must occupy one of the finest sites in England, as there are views all round. At the junction turn right and walk down the hill back to Gumley village, making sure that, on the way, you appreciate the early Victorian weighbridge, the church and the Italianate building that once housed the Gumley Hall stables.

Places of interest nearby
Foxton Locks, just a mile away, is a popular local attraction. A flight of 10 locks, on the Grand Union Canal, is accompanied by an incline, along which a steam-powered boat lift once operated. A museum explains how this worked. *Market Harborough* (4 miles south-east) is an interesting town with medieval buildings. Its suburb, Great Bowden, has the *Frank Haynes Gallery*, with pottery and painting exhibitions.

Dogs allowed in main bar

The Langton Arms

This is a busy and popular pub and deserves to be so. The hospitality is friendly, the atmosphere is traditional, families are welcome, and the food served is excellent. Inside, there are several different bar rooms, arranged around a central bar counter. The decor is olde-worlde in the nicest sense, with large wooden settle seats, ceiling beams, panelled inglenooks with horse brasses, plates and brassware adorning the walls. Open fires burn cosily in winter. Outside, there is a large garden where children's play equipment is provided, as well as the more usual picnic tables and benches.

This is a Marston's house so the real ales offered include Pedigree and Best Bitter. The draught cider is Scrumpy Jack and a full wine list is provided. The menu ranges from light snacks and sandwiches to a varied selection of main meals, with several dishes available for vegetarians. The regular menu cards are supplemented by daily specials and so the choice is always wide-ranging. There are starters like pâtés, dips and savoury pancakes; substantial snacks like filled jacket potatoes and burgers, with or without side salads, and main course options, such as steaks, grills, fish dishes and various pasta or rice concoctions. Cashew nut pearls, or spinach and ricotta ravioli might appeal to vegetarians. Sweets include trifle, cheesecakes, fruit crumbles and home-made puddings.

The Langton Arms keeps normal pub opening times. Special functions and coach parties are catered for, and games evenings and live music events are held.

Telephone: 01858 545278.

How to get there: Church Langton stands on the B6047, 4 miles north of Market Harborough, and can be reached from the A6 at Kibworth Beauchamp. Leicester is 12 miles away to the north-west. The Langton Arms is situated at the southern end of the village.

Parking: There is a large pub car park behind the Langton Arms. Vehicles can also be left along the village roadsides, but preferably not along the B6047 itself.

Length of the walk: 3 miles. OS map: Landranger 141 Kettering and Corby (inn GR 723933).

There are five villages collectively known as 'The Langtons' and many pleasant walks can be enjoyed between all of them. One good circular route takes in West Langton (site of Langton Hall), Tur Langton and the hamlet of Stonton Wyville. This walk, however, links the other Langton settlements, namely East Langton and Thorpe Langton. These are pretty places and should be explored at leisure. The route throughout is clearly marked by signposts and arrow discs. Some stiles need to be climbed and the ground underfoot is generally firm. In many of the fields crossed you will see wonderfully clear examples of ridge-and-furrow markings, indicating ancient sites of Saxon and medieval farming.

The Walk

The route begins immediately next to the Langton Arms, the footpath signpost being located along the drive to the car park. Beyond the stile, walk across the field at an angle, keeping the car park over to your left. A further stile leads through to the next field, at the far side of which is the road. Turn right to reach a T-junction.

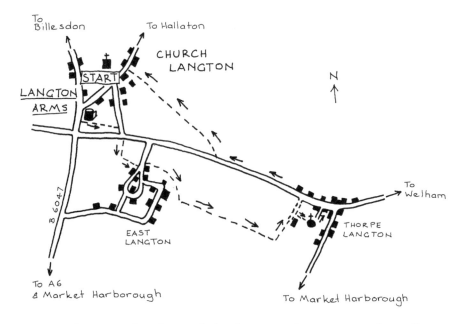

To Billesdon

To Hallaton

CHURCH LANGTON

N

START

LANGTON ARMS

B 6047

EAST LANGTON

THORPE LANGTON

To Welham

To A6 & Market Harborough

To Market Harborough

From there another footpath begins opposite, over another stile. Keeping to the hedgerow, take the first gateway you reach on the left. Cross diagonally the next field, aiming for the houses in the distance. Along by the cricket pitch you eventually meet the road and the edge of East Langton village.

This is a pleasant little place with many old and interesting cottages. Those with a thirst may like to sample the delights of the Bell Inn, which you will find opposite the cricket pavilion, where you emerge onto the road. The footpath to Thorpe Langton officially starts a little way up to the left, alongside Yew Tree Cottage, and continuing round the back garden. Some locals, however, may prefer it, if you reach the path by way of the gateway next to the Bell Inn car park.

From behind the Bell Inn, go diagonally across a large field, keeping the houses of the village to your right-hand side. The views, by this time, have opened out and you can see Thorpe Langton church in the distance. In the bottom corner of the field an arrow disc points the way ahead. The route is clear, as you aim straight for the church spire, walking across a number of fields and climbing several stiles. Gradually the path veers right, and the spire will be seen to your half-left. Soon you reach a gate with an arrow disc pointing left. Go through this gate and follow that direction accordingly, to reach a clear trackway that leads to the road. Before reaching the road, however, turn right along a path across a field to St Leonard's church, a handsome building much restored in Victorian times. This last section of the route, incidentally, forms part of the Leicestershire Round long distance footpath and is signposted as such. Past the church, turn left down a lane to the road. The way back to Church Langton begins along this road, but you should linger awhile and look around Thorpe Langton. The Bakers Arms is the local hostelry.

The road walk is only about ½ mile long. After a slight left bend, you will see a footpath signpost pointing the way right. The route from this point is clear. The path cuts diagonally across two large fields, aiming all the while for the distant church tower. At the far end, walk beside a football pitch and through a school yard to the road. The medieval Church of St Peter is now opposite and those with time should take a look at the interior. It is a fine piece of Gothic architecture. The Langton Arms will be found at the bottom of the road signposted to Foxton and Market Harborough. It will be reached in just a few expectant paces.

Places of interest nearby
The *Hallaton Village Museum* (5 miles north-east) has an exhibition of village life, work and history. At Stockerston (3 miles further east) is *Sweethedges Farm*, where visitors can walk through woods and beside a reservoir, and enjoy bird-watching or fishing. There is also a teashop. At *Kibworth Harcourt* (3 miles west of Church Langton) is an old post mill, complete with sails and machinery.

9 Great Glen
The Crown Inn

In the days when Leicestershire formed part of the Saxon kingdom of Mercia, Great Glen was the site of a royal palace. It is not known where this building could have stood, but some say it might have been close to the river Sence. The Crown Inn stands a little to the east of the river Sence, in the centre of the oldest part of the village. Its name, however, is purely coincidental and has nothing to do with any possible origins to the building's foundations.

That being said, the pub is rather palatial in its proportions. It is very large and the open-plan rooms are extremely spacious. Much of the building is modern, being constructed in a timber chalet style. The ceiling extends into the high pitched roof and the walls are panelled in Scandinavian design. From the main lounge two other large rooms can be reached up flights of steps, and some tables are positioned on mezzanine balconies. At the older end of the building pool tables stand in two further rooms, these being in constant use during the evenings.

Theakston and John Smith's real ales are served. Strongbow and

Woodpecker ciders and various wines are also available. The food is excellent, from bar snacks like ploughman's lunches, sandwiches, burgers and jacket potatoes to main meals like steak, lasagne, fish dishes and items with chips. Special burgers and lasagnes, and a five-bean chilli are among the vegetarian choices.

Normal pub opening times are kept. Children are very welcome; play equipment can be found in the garden and, in one corner of the lounge, a special kiddies corner is set aside.

Telephone: 0116 2592725.

How to get there: Great Glen stands on the A6 between Leicester and Market Harborough, 6 miles south-east of Leicester city centre. The Crown Inn is located on the northern side of the A6, at the eastern end of the village.

Parking: There is a large pub car park. Vehicles should not be left along the A6 itself, but space is available along some of the lanes behind the Crown. Most of the village lies north of the main road.

Length of the walk: 3½ miles. OS map: Landranger 141 Kettering and Corby (inn GR 657975).

Great Glen stands on the river Sence whose valley is extremely attractive. Many footpaths run up and down this valley and these offer many opportunities for good walks, for example, up to Houghton on the Hill and Billesden and down to Wistow and Harcourt, linking up with the Grand Union Canal towpath. This circular walk follows a footpath along a tributary stream of the river Sence to the pretty village of Burton Overy, and returns by bridleways across a countryside much devoted to horses. The route is clear throughout and the paths are generally dry and well worn.

The Walk
From the Crown Inn walk eastwards down the main road. The A6 is busy with traffic, but there is a pavement set into the grass verge, so the walk is safe. Beyond the edge of the village, as the road begins to climb, you will reach a footpath signpost, pointing the way to Burton Overy. This is located just past a cottage called the Old Mill, and the footpath runs down by a hedge behind that building. A stile then takes you into open countryside.

43

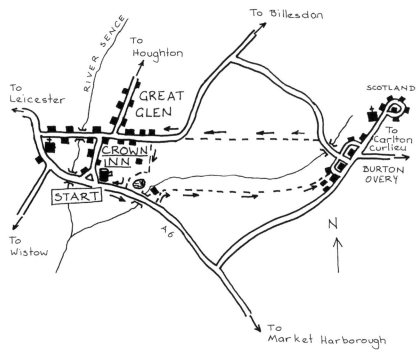

The way to Burton Overy, a distance of just over a mile, is well signposted. At each stile is a yellow-topped post and an arrow disc pointing the way ahead, so there should be no problem in finding your way. All the while, keep to the bottom of the shallow valley, with the stream down to your left and the fields up to your right. At one point a plank bridge carries you across a side stream. Shortly before Burton Overy the footpath veers away from the valley bottom and heads straight for the distant houses. Ignore the sheep track going half-right, and cross diagonally the field to a stile beneath the hedgerow trees on the far side. Beyond this you walk along by a domestic hedge to reach the road. Go straight on, or right then left. Either route will bring you to the village centre.

Burton Overy should be explored before continuing the circular walk. The church is a handsome Gothic edifice dating from the 13th century, while the rectory is early 18th century. Many of the other buildings date from the 17th century. The northern end of the village is called 'Scotland'. This name is not derived from the country, but from the old word 'scot' meaning a tax or shared payment. The fields here might have been rented, or their produce taxed.

The route back to Great Glen begins at the eastern end of Burton Overy, along Washbrook Lane. This can be reached from the Bell pub, down Bell Lane. Beyond the last cottages you cross the stream by a little bridge, then, almost immediately, turn left. A bridleway signpost points the way across the farmland. The grassy track is very clear as it heads westwards through horse paddocks and along field edges. Yellow-topped posts and blue arrow discs mark the route. In due course you reach the road, along which you continue to Great Glen.

The last section is very pleasant. Shortly after the Great Glen name board turn left down another bridleway, this one signposted to London Road. The route goes down across the edge of the first field and half-right diagonally across the second, crossing faint ridge-and-furrow markings, to a gate beneath an ash tree. Thereafter the path heads for the far woodland, through which it goes right then left. Walk beside the lake, then across a field to reach a gate on the far side. From there a gravel track leads down to the main road. Whilst passing the lake be sure to look up to your right for a view of Great Glen Hall. This elegant Regency house, with bow windows and a veranda, is one of the most handsome buildings in the area.

Places of interest nearby

Just 2 miles west in Wistow is *Wiston Le Dale Model Village*, a Victorian re-creation set up in a garden centre. It is $\frac{1}{18}$th of actual size and contains wonderful detail. In the Leicester suburb of Oadby (3 miles north-west) is *Farmworld* at Stoughton Farm Park. This has shire horses, rare breeds and a special children's farmyard.

Dogs allowed downstairs on a lead

⑩ Woodhouse Eaves
The Wheatsheaf Inn

Woodhouse Eaves is not short of watering holes. There is Ye Olde Bulls Head at the northern end of the village, the Forest Rock near the church and The Wheatsheaf at the southern end. This is not surprising, for we are in Charnwood Forest, one of the most attractive parts of the county. The Country Park, which includes Beacon Hill, is close by and Bradgate Park lies a little to the south.

Of the three pubs named, the Wheatsheaf is perhaps the most select and intimate. The single open-plan bar is a lounge and there are no games machines. There are carpets and comfortable chairs, and the walls are hung with hunting pictures and stuffed animals. Outside, in the old coaching yard, tables and benches are laid out on a terrace – a good safe place for children.

The Wheatsheaf prides itself on its selection of real ales and the quality of its food. A blackboard over the bar counter lists the real ales, which may include Ruddles County and Marston's Pedigree, and a blackboard near the door lists the daily specials that supplement the regular items, such as sandwiches, ploughman's lunches, salads and pasta dishes. The daily specials are superb, often featuring chargrilled Angus steaks, salmon, and for vegetarians, such meals as mushroom and nut fettucini. Addlestones draught cider and all manner of wines, including fruit wines, tempt the non-ale drinkers, while home-made bread and butter pudding may tempt those not worried about their waistlines.

The Wheatsheaf Inn keeps normal pub opening times. Telephone: 01509 890320.

How to get there: Woodhouse Eaves is situated 4 miles south of Loughborough, 8 miles east of Coalville and 10 miles north-west of Leicester. It stands between the B591 and B5330, a short distance from junction 22 of the M1 motorway. The Wheatsheaf Inn will be found at Brand Hill, at the southern end of the village.

Parking: There is a large car park at the inn, reached through the coaching entrance arch. Vehicles can also be left along the roadside.

Length of the walk: 2½ miles. OS map: Landranger 129 Nottingham and Loughborough (inn GR 535135).

There are so many walks, of varying lengths, that can be taken from Woodhouse Eaves that the country lover is spoilt for choice. There are designated paths around both the local Country Parks, and forest trails have been laid out in Swithland Wood nearby. Footpaths also link the village with Swithland Reservoir, two miles to the east. This circular walk goes to the sister village of Woodhouse and back, along well worn and well signposted footpaths. The distance given is measured from the church in Woodhouse Eaves. Those wishing to walk from the Wheatsheaf should add a mile to the total.

The Walk
From the church in the centre of the village, the walk begins down Meadow Road. Those driving from the Wheatsheaf can park their cars in one of the side streets, or in the free car park located uphill (north) from the church. At the bottom of Meadow Road is a school and, to its right, a metal gate. Through the gate a clear gravel path leads along by some bushes towards the open countryside. You follow this path for about 100 yards and then bear right,

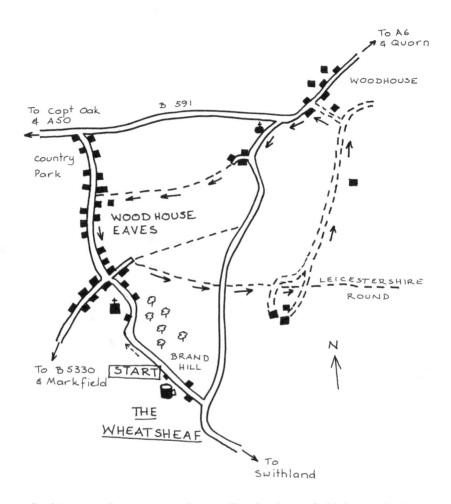

climbing a stile, to cross diagonally the large field beyond. Aim towards the large silo towers of the distant farm. At the far side follow the hedgerow along to the road. The path so far is very clear since it forms part of the Leicestershire Round long distance footpath.

Cross straight over the road and continue along a wide grassy track, bounded by a wire fence each side. The signpost at the road points the way to Swithland Reservoir although, of course, this circuit does not follow this path that far. At the next gate, cross over the wide farm track and stile opposite, then continue along the edge of a field. Climb a further stile onto a tarmac track. To the right is private, leading to a farmstead. Turn left along the bridleway, arrowed to Quorn. This is a pleasant stretch of the walk. On the skyline to the left is Beacon Hill, and away to your right is Buddon Wood. Beyond the thatched house, which is over to your right, turn left with the track, ignoring another bridleway going straight on. Soon you reach Woodhouse. At the road, turn left and then left again when you reach the little church. This takes you down School Lane. At the bottom of the hill, where the road bears left, turn right to walk round by the cottages. A signpost at the corner points the way to Woodhouse Eaves and Forest Road. At the far end a narrow tarmac path continues alongside a stone wall and beneath the trees.

The route back is now clear. Beside the stream, across three fields and through two kissing gates the tarmac path leads you all the way back. The last stretch passes beside a cricket pitch and tennis courts. Beyond these you reach the road. Turn left for the church. Now, perhaps, is the time to wander around the village, admiring the old cottages and their gardens, the early 19th-century church and, should you need refreshment, the various pubs.

Places of interest nearby

At *Wheatsheaf Lodge* (2 miles north) is a Country Walk and Farm Museum, both situated on a working farm. *Stonehurst* at Mountsorrel (3 miles east), is another farm open to the public, this one including a blacksmith's forge and motor museum. From Loughborough to Leicester the *Great Central Railway* runs steam locomotives, with a museum and engine shed, at the Loughborough end.

Dogs allowed downstairs

11 Rearsby
The Horse and Groom

This is a fitting name for an old coaching inn, but the building's central archway now forms the entrance to the car park, not to the stable yard. Nevertheless, this pub remains truly traditional. It has not been modernised with an artificial 'olde worlde' character; this is the real article! Pictures hang above the dado rails, upholstered bench seats surround the walls and the wooden bar counter nestles in a dark corner. There are three small interconnecting rooms; one acts as a public bar, another as a lounge, and the third doubles as a family room. The atmosphere is extremely welcoming and friendly. Back in 1869 a certain 'Nutty' Miles was convicted of throwing a dog and a cat into the open fire. Happily, modern customers are better behaved.

This Ansells pub, which keeps normal opening times, serves a good range of drinks, namely Tetley Bitter, Ansells Bitter and Marston's Pedigree real ales, draught ciders and various wines. However, it is the food on offer which especially attracts customers. It is wholesome, home-cooked and hearty. Prices are

50

reasonable and portions large. Bar snacks include all kinds of sandwiches, jacket potatoes and filled Yorkshire puddings. Main meals feature steaks, pies, lasagnes and curries, while vegetarians are offered various bakes and pasta dishes. Children have their own little menu. Special Sunday lunches are cooked and the mixed grills are locally famous.

The Horse and Groom is reputed to be haunted by the ghost of a previous landlord. It is said he lives down in the cellar, loathe to leave his beloved tavern. And who can blame him?

Telephone: 01664 424242.

How to get there: Rearsby stands on the A607 Syston to Melton Mowbray road, 8 miles north of Leicester and 8 miles south-east of Loughborough. The Horse and Groom is situated on the south side of the main road at the southern edge of the village.

Parking: There is a pub car park, reached through the central arch of the building. Elsewhere, vehicles can be left along the village lanes on the far side of the A607. Parking on the main road should be avoided.

Length of the walk: 3 miles. OS map Landranger 129 Nottingham and Loughborough (inn GR 650142).

This walk is to Ratcliffe on the Wreake and back, across the meadows of the river Wreake. The route is clear throughout, following well trodden paths with frequent signposts and directional arrow discs. There are, however, a few stiles to climb. Part of the return journey is along a section of the Leicestershire Round, a designated long distance footpath that circumnavigates the county. The countryside is very pretty in this part of Leicestershire with rolling hills and winding streams, and the area is rich in wildlife. Rearsby village is worth a closer look, for it has an 18th-century pack-horse bridge, old 'knitting' cottages and a 13th-century church.

The Walk

Turn left outside the Horse and Groom, along the A607, crossing over when traffic permits. A footpath signpost, and a kissing-gate, will soon be seen on the right. Cross the field diagonally in the

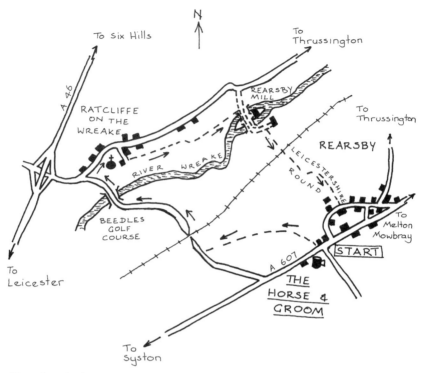

direction indicated by the sign. The path is well worn and clear. In the far corner go over a stile and continue in the same direction across the next field, roughly along the line of telegraph poles. Round the hedgerow, in the next corner, is another stile. Keep to the edge of the next two fields, with the hedgerow on your left, until you reach a final stile, then turn right along the road.

Follow the road for about a mile to reach the village of Ratcliffe on the Wreake. But it is not an unpleasant walk, as the traffic is light and the scenery pleasant. After crossing the railway line, by a level crossing, the road swings left to run alongside the river. Along this stretch of road, a pleasant footpath keeps to the river bank, beneath a line of trees. Beedles Golf Course will be seen over to the left, on the other side of the road. After crossing the bridge over the river Wreake, turn right, following the sign pointing to Thrussington. Ratcliffe on the Wreake is a small village with an attractive mix of old and new houses and a tall-spired church. The cottage gardens are especially pretty.

Immediately beyond the church turn right down Church Lane, then at the far end, go over the stile on the left. The next stretch consists of a series of fields, gates and stiles, through which the path is not always very clearly marked. However, the route should still be fairly obvious. Across the first field (note the ridge-and-furrow markings of old strip-farming systems), aim for the right-hand end of a line of tall trees, where you will find a stile. Continue in the same direction across the next field (keeping the hedge to your left) to a gate. Through this, cross diagonally a small paddock, climb over a stile and continue in same direction, to cross a number of fields and stiles. Aim to the right of the distant farmstead and cross each field diagonally. At one point a wooden paddock fence must be climbed, at another, a plank bridge over a ditch must be crossed. Soon you will see the river Wreake close at hand on the right. At the rough tarmac track turn right to cross the bridge.

The last stretch is easy to follow, as it forms part of the Leicestershire Round route. Follow the rough tarmac track round beside Rearsby Mill and towards Rearsby Mill Cottage. Just before the latter, climb the stile on the right, cross the lawn and climb over the stile on the far side. An earthy track leads onwards between

The pack-horse bridge at Rearsby.

hedgerows (beware nettles), and then across the railway line (beware trains). Beyond, the surface becomes firmer. The track leads you left then right, directly to Rearsby. At Mill Road, turn left to look around the village, or bear right to return to the Horse and Groom.

Places of interest nearby
At Syston (3 miles south-west) is the 230-acre *Watermead Country Park*, complete with nature reserve, woodland walks and a picnic area. Near Barkby (4 miles further south) is the deserted village of *Hamilton*, the house and street outlines still visible in the fields.

12 Ashby Folville
The Carington Arms

Dogs allowed during day if well-behaved

This attractive and well known pub certainly enjoys a lovely setting, positioned opposite the cricket pitch in a quiet and pretty village. The Smith-Carington family has owned most of the land and buildings around here since the 16th century, and we must be grateful to them for keeping the beauty of the place intact.

The Carington Arms is not an especially old building, but it is very traditional. The interior is comfortable and cosy, with wooden furniture, dado rail and old photographs of the village decorating the walls. There is one long large room, which is sub-divided into sections; one end acting as the public bar, the other used as a dining area. Beyond the latter you will find a no smoking room. There is also a skittle alley, together with a function room used for special occasions. Dominating the main bar is a central open fire with a free-standing copper chimney hood; wonderful to sit around in winter months. In summer, the large garden, furnished with children's play equipment, is popular.

This Everards house opens normal pub times and serves

numerous real ales including Everards Old Original and Tiger. The draught cider is Scrumpy Jack and various wines are offered. The menus are wide-ranging, with regular items being supplemented by daily specials written up on blackboards. Snacks include sandwiches, ploughman's lunches, burgers and salads; main meals range from steak, meat pies and fish dishes to curries and pasta. Children have their own menu. Vegetarians can choose from cheese bakes, vegetable lasagnes and nut based dishes. Desserts change daily but may include various cakes and pastries.

Telephone: 01664 840228.

How to get there: Ashby Folville stands 2 miles north-west of Twyford on the B674 , in the heart of lovely, unspoilt hill country between Leicester and Melton Mowbray. It is 6 miles from Leicester. The Carington Arms will be found at the western end of the village.

Parking: There is a large pub car park. Vehicles can also be left along the village lanes provided no obstruction is caused. The lane running north from the Carington Arms is a 'no through road' and this provides parking space.

Length of the walk: 3½ miles. OS map: Landranger 129 Nottingham and Loughborough (inn GR 707122).

Ashby Folville – named after the Folville family that ruled this area in the 14th century – remains an estate village. This means that the landscape around the village is attractively maintained in 'parkland' character, with avenues of trees and lawned vistas. In consequence, very pleasant walks can be enjoyed in all directions. This circuit takes in the attractive villages of Gaddesby and Barsby, both well worth an inquisitive wander around. The outward route keeps to the Leicestershire Round long distance footpath, the return follows less well-marked paths. There are stiles to climb, but nothing should be too difficult.

The Walk

Walk down Highfield End, the dead-end lane that runs north from the Carington Arms, and then left along the footpath signposted to Gaddesby. This will be found immediately beyond Harewell Cottages. The path leads you beside some back gardens to a stile,

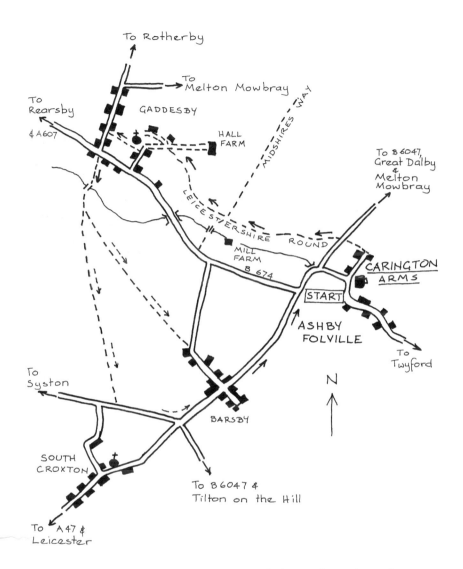

upon which yellow arrow discs are nailed up. These show the way. The route to Gaddesby is, in fact, well marked since it is part of the designated Leicestershire Round footpath. Most of the gates or stiles along its route have yellow arrow discs pointing the way ahead. At the top corner of the first field a stile leads onto a road. Cross over this and continue on the far side, the path leading

An ancient 'cruck' house in Barsby village.

diagonally half-left across a field. Through the following field the spire of Gaddesby church should be visible (half-right), sticking up above the distant trees. Continue over more stiles, across more fields and, at one point, over a plank bridge. Soon you will notice that Gaddesby spire is directly ahead and the stream is directly to your left. Mill Farm is also on your left, further away.

In due course, you cross over a clear track that forms part of the Midshires Way, a designated route that passes through much of the East Midlands, including the shire counties of foxhunting fame. There are more stiles and plank bridges to negotiate as you continue westwards. In the field beyond the Midshires Way you should notice the signs of ridge-and-furrow, remnants of old strip-farming. Keeping the Hall Farm complex over to your right, cross the last two fields diagonally. Emerging onto the end of the drive that leads back to Hall Farm, and turning left along it, you soon reach the church. Continue along a footpath beyond to reach the main part of the village. Those with time available should explore Gaddesby, for it is a pretty spot.

The route to Barsby, which starts almost opposite the Cheney Arms on the main road, is not wonderfully clear since it uses footpaths that cross a number of large fields. Stiles, arrow discs and yellow-topped posts are provided to mark the way, but these tend to be situated far apart. From the footpath signpost, a gravel tree-lined track runs down to a wooden bridge across the river. From the far side of this, two footpaths continue, one to the left, another to the half-left. Either can be followed, the former being the shorter of the two routes. This cuts diagonally across the farmland aiming directly for the distant houses. The longer route passes the end of a line of poplar trees, crosses a large field to a plank bridge and then continues in the same direction, eventually to cross a shallow valley. Keeping the farmstead over to the left this path reaches the road, which is then followed to the left.

Barsby is a quiet little place with some interesting cottages, one of which is a conversion from a brick-built church. The King William pub can be visited, if opening times suit. Ashby Folville is easily reached, by following the lane running north. A pavement is provided the whole way and the views across the Folville estate are very pleasant.

Places of interest nearby
Melton Mowbray (6 miles north-east) is a bustling town with a street market twice a week, a museum and the Melton Country Park. At *Burrough Hill Country Park* there is an Iron Age hill fort affording spectacular views all around.

Dogs allowed only in bar area

(13) Knossington
The Fox and Hounds

In the 18th century this was a popular coaching inn, serving travellers on the Oakham to Leicester road. Today, it is still a popular pub, but Knossington has long ceased to be a major centre. The old coaching road has declined in importance, and with it the settlements along its route have fallen back into a sleepy, unrushed existence.

The Fox and Hounds has obviously remained popular because it is friendly, welcoming, cosy and unpretentious. It caters for walkers, families, tourists and locals, and serves an excellent range of food and drink. Inside, there is one main bar sub-divided into three small sections; one houses the pool table, another forms the public bar, the third being used as a lounge. Upholstered settle benches line the wooden dado walls, which are adorned with hunting prints, plates, horse brasses and copperware.

Belonging to Ascot Estates, the Fox and Hounds sells Courage real ales. It also offers Scrumpy Jack draught cider and various wines from different European countries. But it is the home-made and excellent value food that best recommends the place. There are bar snacks, such as jacket potatoes, beans on toast and burgers, as well as main meals like steaks, lemon sole and chilli con carne. Vegetarian specials include vegetable stroganoff. In summer months, weather permitting, barbecues are held at weekends.

The Fox and Hounds opens normal pub times. No doubt the customers would prefer more time to enjoy the convivial atmosphere.

Telephone: 01664 454676.

How to get there: Knossington is situated in the far east of Leicestershire, close to the border with Rutland, and only 4 miles from Oakham. Approaching from the Leicester direction, the village is best reached from Tilton-on-the-Hill, which stands on the B6047. The Fox and Hounds will be found opposite the church.

Parking: There is a pub car park. Vehicles can easily be left elsewhere in the village (with due respect for locals), since the lanes here are very quiet.

Length of the walk: 3½ miles. OS map: Landranger 141 Kettering and Corby (inn GR 802087).

Knossington is set amidst some of the loveliest countryside in Leicestershire; an open, unpopulated landscape of broad valleys and dense woodlands. The lanes all around are generally empty and offer good walking routes. Launde Abbey is within walking distance (3 miles south), so too are the abbey ruins at Owston (2 miles west). This circular walk includes a bridleway that heads in the Launde Abbey direction and a footpath that runs alongside Owston Woods. The views throughout are excellent. The route is clearly marked and well worn, following tracks and field edges. A few stiles are encountered, but there is little to cause any difficulty.

The Walk

Go downhill from the Fox and Hounds and turn left along Main Street. Then take the second right turn, Braunston Road, and head south away from the village. A bridleway will soon be reached; a waymarked track on the right-hand side of the road that begins at a gate next to a lone house. You follow this bridleway for more than

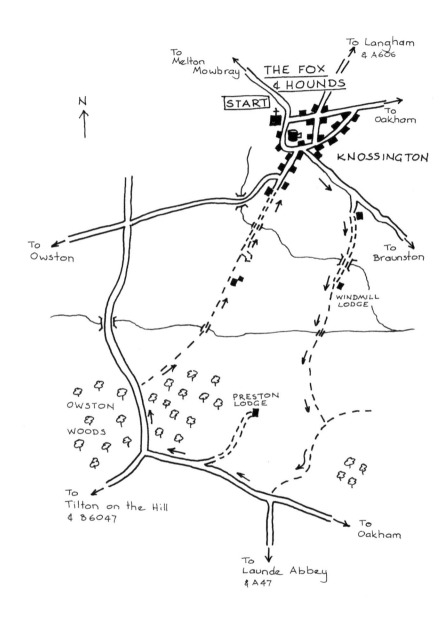

To Langham
& A606

THE FOX
& HOUNDS

To Melton
Mowbray

START

N

To Oakham

KNOSSINGTON

To Owston

To Braunston

WINDMILL
LODGE

OWSTON

WOODS

PRESTON
LODGE

To Oakham

To
Tilton on the Hill
& B6047

To Launde Abbey
& A47

a mile, all the way in fact to the Tilton to Oakham road. The way is very clear and little description is necessary of the exact route. Simply enjoy the surroundings, from the ridge-and-furrow markings in some of the fields and the numerous hedgerows full of wildlife, to the delightful views across Leicestershire.

The trackway curves a little, crosses a stream and climbs to a farmhouse called Windmill Lodge. Beyond this it disappears for a short stretch, so aim for the distant, left-hand corner of the pasture field, which will be visible almost straight ahead. Beyond the next gate the rutted trackway reappears as it climbs up a grassy slope, then continues southwards by the edges of several fields. On meeting another track, bear right and go through a double farm gate. Keeping the hedgerow to your left proceed ahead. In due course a dip down and a curve round to the right brings you up to the road. Only the occasional horse may have passed you on this whole stretch of bridleway. Fittingly perhaps, because it is thought this was once the route used by medieval horse caravans as they carried produce to and from Launde Abbey.

Launde Abbey can be reached down the lane opposite the point you reach the road, and those with time should make the detour to see it. Now used as a Diocese Retreat House, the old monastic buildings have been incorporated into a fine 17th-century manor house.

The circular walk continues down the road westwards, to the right as you reach it from the bridleway. In due course, turn right again along the road signposted to Knossington. This is a quiet lane, which winds up and round through Owston Woods. The deciduous trees form a tall canopy and, on either side, forest wildlife may be seen and heard. The footpath back to Knossington begins on the right, just beyond Owston Woods, where the road bends left. A wooden pedestrian gate will be found half-hidden in the hedgerow. Aim straight ahead across the middle of the field, keeping distant Knossington in front and the woodland edge down to the right. Across a shallow valley the path continues through fields and over stiles. The stream is crossed by a well made wooden bridge with handrail, and the edges of several fields are followed, with the hedgerow to the right. Beyond some farm buildings, and over the brow of the next hill, you join a rutted track. This leads onwards down into the next valley and then up to the village on the skyline. The Fox and Hounds will be reached by turning right at the road and then left at the junction.

Knossington church.

Places of interest nearby

Near Tilton-on-the-Hill (4 miles south-west) is *Halstead House Farm and Nature Trail* where visitors can walk round a working farm and along the line of an old railway track. Just 2 miles further east is *Sauvey Castle* where remnants of a motte-and-bailey castle can be seen on the banks of the river Chater. Those interested in more recent archaeology can visit the *John O'Gaunt Viaduct* (4 miles west), a 14-arch brick structure that no longer carries the railway line built in 1878.

14 Waltham on the Wolds
The Royal Horse Shoes

Not in evening but allowed during day if no-one is eating

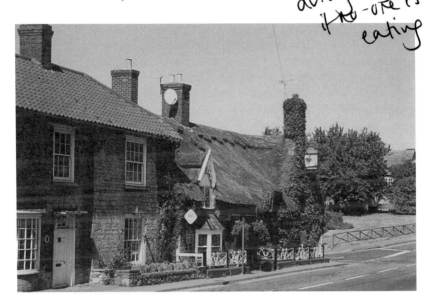

Waltham on the Wolds is not only a large village, but a pretty one, with a gathering of old buildings clustered around the church. It is set in attractive hill country, hence the village name; the Wolds consisting of a limestone escarpment. To the west is the Vale of Belvoir, merging with the Midland plain; to the east is Fen country.

The Royal Horse Shoes is a fine old thatched building, dating back to the 17th century. Inside all is traditional, with low ceiling beams, panelled walls, open fireplaces and various pictures and prints with a strong hunting theme adorn the walls. This area, of course, is part of the Belvoir Hunt territory and horses figure prominently in the local lifestyles.

It is a very popular pub and can become very busy. Fortunately, it is also a fairly large establishment. The public bar occupies one end, but most of the space is taken up by an open-plan lounge, this being sub-divided by a central partition and fish tank. Various real ales are served, such as John Smith's Bitter, Ruddles Bitter and Marston's Pedigree. Dry Blackthorn is also available on draught and various wines are offered, either by the glass or bottle. However, it is the food that makes the Royal Horse Shoes exceptional. The range of dishes is wide and the quality is excellent, with regular menu items being supplemented by daily specials. From bar snacks like sandwiches, soup and pâté to main meals like steak, meat pies, lasagne, chicken and curry, the choice is mouth-watering. The fresh fish dishes, in particular salmon and trout, are very popular, whilst vegetarians can order such items as aubergine in tomato sauce and deep-fried Brie. Normal pub opening times are kept.

Telephone: 01664 464289.

How to get there: Waltham on the Wolds is located on the A607 Melton Mowbray to Grantham road, 6 miles from Melton Mowbray. The Royal Horse Shoes will be found at the central crossroads, opposite the church.

Parking: There is a car park at the rear of the pub, reached from the lane to Eastwell. Vehicles can also be left at the roadside along the lane to Stonesby opposite. Parking on the main road should be avoided.

Length of the walk: 2½ miles. OS map: Landranger 130 Grantham (inn GR 802251).

There are many fine walks in this area, and the footpaths are generally well signposted. At Goadby Marshwood, less than 2 miles away west, the Jubilee Way long distance footpath can be joined. This follows a wooded ridge to Belvoir Castle. Beyond Saltby (3 miles east) is the Viking Way long distance footpath, which follows an ancient trackway, now known as The Drift, along the Leicestershire/Lincolnshire border. This short circular walk gives just a taste of the Wolds scenery. It explores Waltham and includes a local viewpoint, now also used by a radio mast. The route is clear and only a few stiles are encountered along the way.

The Walk

From the Royal Horse Shoes walk south down the main road, in the direction of Melton Mowbray. The village stretches along this busy road, but there is a pavement, so the route is safe (if a little noisy). Beyond the primary school the road takes a long gradual

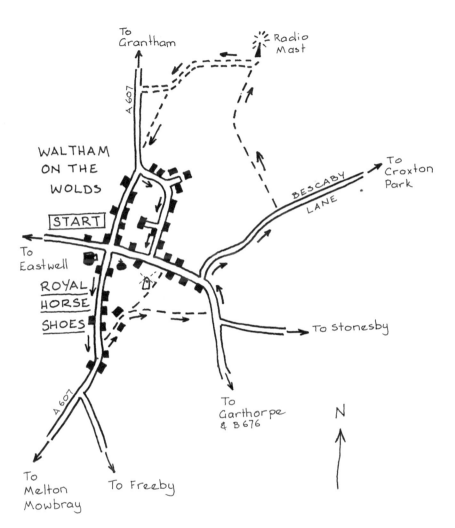

bend to the left. Further on it bends right, but before then, you will see a footpath signpost on the left, close to some bungalows. This points diagonally across a field, behind the village and towards a group of farm buildings. It also labels the route as the Mowbray Way, which was designated in 1994 to mark the centenary of the local parish councils. It is a fairly short 'long distance' footpath and this circuit only follows it to the eastern end of Waltham village.

Keeping the large metal barn to your left, you will shortly reach

Waltham village.

a stile in the far corner of the farmyard complex, where two arrow discs point the way ahead. Disregard the path half-left towards the old windmill, and instead, proceed straight on towards the top corner of the field. A stile leads through to the next field. Follow the edge of this, eventually to reach the road at the eastern edge of the village. More stiles need to be climbed at that point. Turn left and, soon after, head right up Bescaby Lane.

The landscape now begins to open out, as you leave the village behind. Bescaby Lane is, in fact, a 'no through road'. Two miles further north it ends in Croxton Park, now a private estate but once the site of a medieval monastery. This circuit, however, leaves the lane after just ½ mile, a few hundred yards beyond the Bescaby Landfill Site. A clear footpath on the left, leads across a field and then, beyond the far hedgerow, along by a field edge to the National Air Traffic Services Grantham Radio Station. The route is perfectly clear, as the aerial tower can be seen for miles around!

Around the perimeter fence is a large gravel parking area, marking the entrance to the Belvoir Estate. Beyond the stone walls and gates are the grass and all-weather gallops, much used by the local horse-owning fraternity. You can walk through this area, along a public bridleway, but this particular circuit turns east at this point to head back to Waltham. The views all around are broad and open, and to the north you can see deep into Lincolnshire.

The tarmac lane first bends left, then right. At the second bend continue straight on, diagonally across a field along the line of a bridleway. At the main road turn left for the village centre. To avoid the traffic, bear left at the edge of Waltham along Mere Road and then, at the far end, turn left then right along Burgins Lane. This leads directly to the church.

Places of interest nearby

Melton Mowbray (6 miles south) has various attractions, including *Melton Country Park*, *Melton Market* and many old and interesting shops, including *Ye Olde Pork Pie Shoppe* where traditional pork pies are made in front of visitors. At Colsterworth in Lincolnshire (8 miles east) is *Woolsthorpe Manor*, birthplace of Sir Isaac Newton.

Dogs allowed.

15 Redmile
The Peacock Inn

closed for refurbishment until 21/3/03

Just 2 miles from Belvoir Castle, Redmile is a village of great character. It has an interesting mixture of medieval and Victorian buildings and two excellent pubs, the Windmill and the Peacock. The streets seem ever busy, especially with walkers and tourists, and the place exudes a happy, friendly atmosphere. The name, incidentally, comes from 'red mould' (red earth).

The Peacock Inn opens all day and well it might for it is a very popular, and delightfully old, pub serving a wide range of food and drink. Children are welcome at all times and throughout the building. Inside, the 17th-century character has been preserved and all is dark, cosy and comfortable. Apart from a separate restaurant, there are six small rooms set around a central bar counter. Low ceiling beams, brick and stone fireplaces with wood-burning stoves, panelled walls and country-style ornaments enhance the relaxing ambience. The furniture consists of wooden kitchen tables and treadle sewing machine conversions, settles and settees. All very fascinating, and comfortable.

The Peacock prides itself on its beer selection, with various real ales available on draught, like Marston's Pedigree, Greene King Abbot Ale and regularly changing guest brews. Strongbow cider and various wines are also offered. But the range of food served is even more impressive – and what quality! French provincial cooking is *de rigueur*, on both the regular menu and the list of daily specials written up on the blackboard. Bar snacks include French bread sandwiches, soups, pâté, moules and Stilton soufflé; main meals might feature salmon, steak, venison, duck and pasta dishes. Vegetarians may choose from spaghetti with vegetables and ginger, vegetable cannelloni, or mushroom risotto. There is a wide cheese selection and all manner of fruit and cream desserts.

Telephone: 01949 842554.

How to get there: Redmile is situated in the far north-east corner of the county in the Vale of Belvoir, 8 miles east of Grantham. The nearest main roads are the A607 Melton Mowbray to Grantham road and the A52 Nottingham to Grantham road. The Peacock Inn stands next to the church.

Parking: There is only a small pub car park, but vehicles can easily be left along the village streets, provided no obstruction is caused. Nearby Church Lane offers a quiet thoroughfare for parking and there is a little car park near the canal, sited on the old wharf.

Length of the walk: 3½ miles. OS map: Landranger 129 Nottingham and Loughborough (inn GR 796355).

The Grantham Canal passes through Redmile and offers excellent walking opportunities. The towpath can be followed in both directions, across a landscape which is rich in wildlife. Indeed, the canalside eastwards is now a nature reserve. The Jubilee Way long distance footpath runs along the ridge, 2 miles away, that ends at Belvoir Castle itself. From that ridge superb views can be enjoyed in all directions. This circular walk, however, follows the Grantham Canal westwards to the village of Barkestone-le-Vale and then returns across open farmland. It is a very easy walk to follow. A few stiles are encountered but the ground is firm throughout.

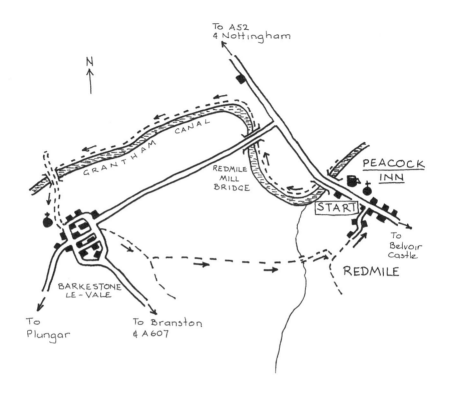

The Walk

The Grantham Canal is just yards away from the Peacock Inn, running through the western edge of the village. Up the road beside the pub you reach the canal bridge, on the right-hand side of which is the way down to the towpath. The walk along the Grantham Canal, westwards, is splendid. For much of this stretch, the canal and towpath run along the top of an embankment, affording good views across the Vale of Belvoir into Nottinghamshire. Since the canal is no longer used by water traffic, the wildlife to be seen is exceptionally varied. Swans and herons nest here, and moorhens, coots and ducks swim amongst the reeds.

The Grantham Canal, 33 miles long and linking Grantham with Nottingham, opened in 1793 and closed in 1929. It is now disused in the sense that some of the bridges have been blocked, and some of the canal-bank trees have grown across the basin, but it is not abandoned. British Waterways still own it and much of the water

72

remains. The towpath has been widened into a grassy thoroughfare, as a result of the good work undertaken by the Grantham Canal Trust and the Grantham Canal Restoration Society. The canal declined in the 19th century as the railway took over much of its traffic. That line survives, through Bingham to Nottingham, but ironically another railway line in these parts did not. The Melton Mowbray line ran alongside this stretch of Grantham Canal, but now is totally dismantled. The fine Redmile Station building, however, can still be seen, close to the Redmile Mill Bridge.

Beyond Redmile Mill Bridge, about a mile further on at bridge Number 51, you leave the towpath. Walk up to the gravel track and then south to the village of Barkestone-le-Vale. Passing the church, on your right, continue down Jericho Lane to the main road junction. From here you have a choice of routes. The way back to Redmile begins at the eastern end of the village, along Fishpond Lane. But the village lanes are in grid pattern (a result of medieval town planning). You can either go left then right, or straight on then left. Those with time, and a thirst, may like to visit the Chequers pub, should it be open.

Stables at Barkestone-le-Vale.

The footpath signpost will be found opposite the end of Middle Lane. The route is clear and marked by arrow discs at each stile. For most of the way you can see Redmile church spire ahead and Belvoir Castle on the skyline to the right, a splendid scene. Cross the first two fields diagonally, to a plank bridge across a ditch, and then cross the middle of the next field to another plank bridge. Two more fields are then crossed diagonally, until you reach the bottom of a combe, near a small sewage works. Beyond the stream, a further stile leads to a path that ends at the bottom of Church Lane. Follow this as it winds all the way back to the Peacock Inn.

Places of interest nearby
Belvoir Castle should not be missed. Home of the Dukes of Rutland, it has fine state rooms, a military museum and grounds with wonderful views. At Plungar (2 miles south-west) is *Our Little Farm*, where a traditional Victorian farmyard contains rare animal breeds.

16 South Luffenham
The Boot and Shoe Inn

Dogs allowed No problems.

Nestling in the heart of an old and interesting village, this pub attracts customers from far and wide. It is a lovely, traditional inn where a wide range of food and drink is served in cosy, welcoming surroundings. Children are catered for – there is a family room – and the popular games room-cum-public bar attracts the dedicated locals. There are also separate areas acting as lounge and dining room. There are oak beams, exposed stone walls hung with prints and horse brasses, and comfortable furniture, including some wonderfully cushioned settees. In winter months open fires warm the bars, while in summer barbecues are a popular feature.

This Pubmaster establishment offers a range of real ales, including Marston's Pedigree and Morland Old Speckled Hen, plus Red Rock draught cider and all manner of wines, from house red and white to the best that Europe can make. A large menu book lists the food available, this being supplemented by daily specials written up on the blackboard. And what a choice! Bar snacks range from sandwiches, jacket potatoes (both with various fillings) and burgers to soups and salads; main meals include home-made meat pies, steaks and numerous fish dishes. Trout and game are served in season, and vegetarians are offered such delicacies as mushroom and nut fettucine.

Outside there are two paved areas laid out as beer gardens. In good weather superstitious customers may prefer to sit here, as the interior is said to be haunted. If a light suddenly goes on or off, or if a door suddenly opens or closes, you may not be alone!

The Boot and Shoe Inn keeps normal pub opening times. Telephone: 01780 720177.   *)) —))*

How to get there: South Luffenham stands on the A6121 Uppingham to Stamford road, just 3 miles south of Rutland Water. The Boot and Shoe Inn will be found off the main road, next to the church whose tall, crocketed spire can be seen for miles around.

Parking: There is a pub car park, reached from Hall Lane. Vehicles can also be parked around the village, provided no obstruction is caused. The streets are narrow and circuitous but are also very quiet.

Length of the walk: 3 miles (4½ mile longer option). OS map: Landranger 141 Kettering and Corby (inn GR 942019).

This circular walk links the large, rambling and ancient villages of South and North Luffenham. They possess a wealth of old and interesting buildings, two fine Gothic churches and four excellent taverns. Both places should be explored at leisure. The route is very pleasant and is easily followed. The footpaths are well signposted and well used, and the ground underfoot is generally firm. There are, however, some stiles to negotiate but these should cause no problem. The views throughout are excellent. As you cross the valley of the river Chater the hills of southern Rutland stretch all around.

The Walk

From outside the front of the pub, turn left to walk alongside the churchyard wall. Soon the road widens into a triangle, where there stands an old red telephone box, and a footpath signpost in the far corner. Follow the direction indicated, down a tarmac path. The village of South Luffenham is divided into two parts; the older part around the church and, across the valley where sheep graze, the

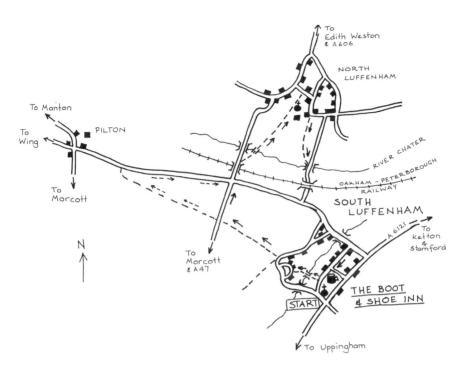

newer end that grew up with the development of the railway line in 1850. It is, of course, the former which is the more interesting. There is a network of narrow lanes, old stone cottages, farmhouses and a house that was once a tithe barn.

The tarmac path that begins the circuit in fact links the two parts of the village. It dips down, crosses the stream and rises up again to reach a little corner called The Square. Here there are some attractive little cottages and a farm. Continue uphill, either left along Frisby Lane and then right, or proceed straight on up Angle Lane and then turn left. Both routes will bring you to the top corner of the village, where Back Lane runs over a bridge (high above the cutting of the deserted railway line) and then bears right. At the bend a signpost will be seen. To the left is a footpath to Morcott, straight on is a bridleway to Pilton. Follow the latter route.

The way is very clear as it crosses the middle of the first large field and follows the edge of the second. Views begin to open out; to your right is North Luffenham, away to the left is the tall windmill, complete with sails, that stands above Morcott. In due

The Hall, North Luffenham.

course, go through a farm gate and continue along a wide hedged trackway until you reach the road. This trackway continues temptingly on the far side of the road but you turn right, aiming for North Luffenham. The trackway that you leave is, in fact, an ancient route. In medieval times it was the main road to Pilton. You can follow it if you wish, but this detour would add 1½ miles to your circuit.

Walk down the road, straight on at the junction and over the Oakham to Peterborough railway line. Almost immediately beyond the bridge take the footpath signposted to the right. This crosses two fields diagonally, taking you across the Chater valley to North Luffenham church. The Hall, once known as Digby Manor House, will be seen to the right as you approach the church. It is a fine 16th-century building which was remodelled in the 19th century. The gardens surrounding it are very pretty, and may be glimpsed through the gateways as you walk through the village.

After passing the church, turn right down Church Street and right again, at the Horse and Panniers public house, down Chapel Lane. At the far corner you will find the 17th-century arch that leads to the grounds of North Luffenham Hall. If you are lucky the wooden doors will stand open, affording a view inside. The route back is now easy. Follow the footpath signposted beside the gateway. This takes you through a metal gate, beside a wall, over a stile and down into the valley across a field.

In the bottom left-hand corner, a stile and plank bridge take you onward to meet the road diagonally. Turn right to go over the river, pass under the railway and then keep left for South Luffenham. The most pleasant way back to the Boot and Shoe Inn, but not the only way, is down Gatehouse Lane. This leads on down Pinfold Lane, across the valley and back to the old part of the village. Turn right down 'The Street' to reach your destination.

Places of interest nearby

The town of *Uppingham* (5 miles west) should not be missed. It has an old market place, several second-hand bookshops and a famous public school. Tours are given of the latter, which boasts a Tudor library and Victorian chapel. *Lyddington Bede House* (2 miles further south) dates from the 15th century and is held by English Heritage. Across the border into Northamptonshire are *Wakerley Woods* (forest trails), and – towards Corby – is the Tudor ruin of *Kirby Hall*.

Dogs allowed on leads

17 Manton
The Horse and Jockey

This pub is a great favourite amongst cyclists, who stop here when undertaking the circuit of Rutland Water. Walkers and motorists also come here, for there is some lovely scenery to be enjoyed and Manton is a pretty, stone-built village.

The Horse and Jockey is justly popular for it is a friendly and cosy place, where good food and drink can be enjoyed in traditional surroundings. Indeed, the interior is traditional country-style, rather than 'olde worlde' in the modern, rather artificial sense. All the decor is unpretentious; horse brasses hang on the beams, jugs stand on the high plate shelf and pictures of horses cover the plain walls. There are two rooms, a public bar with dartboard and a lounge. The furniture in the latter is rather more comfortable than that in the former. Children are welcome, and the benches outside offer a safe rest area on hot days, since the pub stands well away from any busy road.

Mansfield Brewery's Old Baily and Riding Bitter are the real ales on offer, as is the usual selection of stouts, wines and draught cider.

But it is the food served that most satisfies the hungry wayfarer. Large portions and home-cooking attract customers from far afield. With snacks like sandwiches, filled rolls, salads and items with chips, and meals like steak and mushroom pie, haddock pasta with prawns and mushrooms and chilli con carne, no one should go hungry. For vegetarians, the choice includes broccoli and cheese bake and macaroni cheese.

The Horse and Jockey keeps normal pub opening times. Telephone: 01572 737335.

How to get there: Manton stands on the south-western shores of Rutland Water, just 3 miles south of Oakham and 4 miles north of Uppingham. The village centre lies to the east of the A6003. The Horse and Jockey will be found at the northern end of the village, turning left as you approach from the main road.

Parking: There is no pub car park but ample parking space is available along the roadside in front. Cars can also be left along the no through road that runs down the western side of the building.

Length of the walk: 2 miles (3 miles longer option). OS map: Landranger 141 Kettering and Corby (inn GR 878046).

Rutland Water is said to be one of the largest man-made lakes in Europe, yet it sits in England's smallest county – which all seems rather unfair. Be that as it may, the area is now an important water and leisure resource, providing facilities for fishing, sailing and cycling. There are numerous car parks, picnic sites and nature trails, and a Visitor Centre has been built. At the western end, near Manton, is the Lyndon Nature Reserve. This stroll is for nature lovers, since it follows a route to a couple of observation hides – waterside shelters set up for bird-watchers. Binoculars should be taken, together, perhaps, with a bird book. The walk can be extended to the Lyndon Visitor Centre.

The Walk

Turn left outside the Horse and Jockey and walk down St Marys Road to the church. Turn left again, to continue eastwards along Priory Road, which is signposted as a no through road for vehicles. At the far end a farm gate leads you through to open countryside

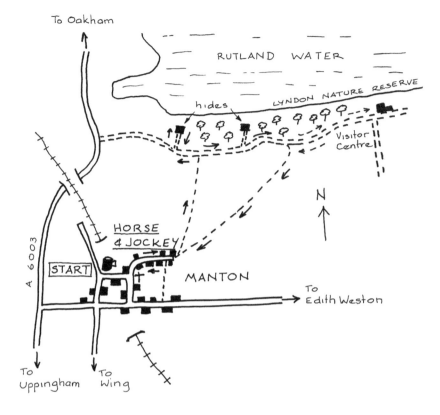

and Rutland Water can be seen down to the left.

The easy way down to the reservoir is along the rutted trackway
that curves down along a line of young trees. However, as this is
used for the return journey, an alternative route has been chosen, to
enable the walk to be circular. Therefore, turn left almost
immediately beyond the gate and cut across the field downhill
towards the waters' edge, keeping the back gardens of the houses to
your left-hand side. The footpath is not clear but this is a right of
way. Go through a gate and continue down across the next field to
the far hedgerow. At a suitable spot, climb the fence to reach the
main shoreline track and turn left.

Where the shoreline track ends at a locked gate turn right to
reach the first hide – Shallow Water Hide. To visit the other hide,
called Water Scrape Hide, retrace your steps along the shoreline
track, and then continue eastwards until a grassy path leads north.

Incidentally, this section of Rutland Water's shoreline track is not actually next to the waters' edge. Instead, it winds attractively along by some willow trees, which rather block the view. However, from the hides themselves many hours of bird-watching can be enjoyed, as the views from these are across the lake.

Well over 200 species of birds have been recorded at Rutland Water, including native wildfowl, migrants and seabirds. In winter mallard, teal and shoveler ducks are seen, as well as divers like pochard. Scaup and goosander may be spotted, along with wigeon, coots and greylag geese. Bewick swans sometimes land here from Siberia, and the occasional migrating osprey may be seen fishing on the lake. In spring and summer there are breeding birds like the great crested grebe, woodpecker, kestrel and redshank.

The return from Water Scrape Hide can be made by continuing along the shoreline track eastwards, to a point where the trees end and the pathway kinks. From there you can turn sharp right and go through a gateway into the adjoining field. Proceed across this, walk uphill diagonally to the top corner, where you enter the next field. Through this a rutted track leads up along the line of trees mentioned earlier. Those wishing to extend their walk should

Manton Village.

continue to the Lyndon Visitor Centre, keeping to the shoreline track for another ½ mile. This was opened in 1984 and offers interesting displays showing the variety of wildlife to be seen in this area.

Places of interest nearby
Near Edith Weston (3 miles east) is the *Normanton Church Water Museum*. Here an elegant classical-style church, preserved from flooding and perched on an embanked peninsula, has been transformed into an exhibition display showing the work of Anglian Water, and its management of Rutland Water. The nearby towns of *Oakham* and *Uppingham* should also be visited, as both have many old buildings and family attractions.

18 Hambleton
The Finch's Arms

No Dogs

Once a hilltop village called Upper Hambleton, this attractive little settlement has, since 1974, been located on an 'island'. Rutland Water lies all around and Hambleton is connected to the mainland by a single road and causeway. A sad isolation for a place that was once a regional Saxon capital. Notwithstanding this fact, Hambleton is a very busy and popular village, with good lake views. Cyclists, walkers, anglers and sailing enthusiasts – not to mention bird-watchers – all come here, especially in the summer months. The Finch's Arms plays host to most of them.

It is a most friendly, welcoming pub, and should not really be missed. The main bar room is traditionally decorated, old pictures of local scenes and wooden furniture complementing the low ceiling beams and stone fireplaces. The back dining room leads out to a terrace overlooking Rutland Water. When the weather is fine customers enjoy sitting in the front and back gardens.

Real ales from the Oakham brewery and Greene King Abbot Ale and IPA are served, together with Dry Blackthorn cider, interesting fruit wines and various stouts and lagers. The menus are equally wide-ranging; from crusty baguettes and ploughman's lunches to steak and kidney pie, roast pheasant and lemon sole. Vegetarians can choose between pasta or vegetable bakes. Daily specials are written up on a large blackboard and there is always a wide selection of desserts, including ice creams.

The Finch's Arms keeps to normal pub opening times but – not surprisingly – these hours are extended somewhat during summer weekends.

Telephone: 01572 756575.

How to get there: Hambleton is not difficult to find, as it is in the middle of Rutland Water. It is reached from the A606, a mile east of Oakham. The Finch's Arms lies opposite the church at the western end of the village.

Parking: There is a large pub car park. Vehicles can also be left by the roadside in the main part of the village. There is also a public car park a short distance westwards, at the beginning of the Hambleton Peninsula Cycle Route.

Length of the walk: 4 miles (shorter options). OS map: Landranger 141 Kettering and Corby (inn GR 900077).

This is a splendid walk which can be enjoyed by people of all ages, despite the distance. The route is easy to follow and the ground underfoot is dry and firm. The Hambleton Peninsula – as the 'island' is called – is circumnavigated, the shoreline cycle track being used almost the whole way round. Rutland Water is thus viewed from all angles. In summer months yachts and water-skiers provide constant interest, while in winter the lake is a favourite haunt for wildfowl. The circuit length can be reduced a little by those wishing to walk only the north or the south shore, the Peninsula road being used as a convenient short-cut route.

The Walk

To reach the shoreline cycle track you can either turn right outside the Finch's Arms, and walk down the road to the main entrance and car park, or else turn left. The latter route involves a footpath across a field. Beyond a house called The Old Stables, on the left, is a gate

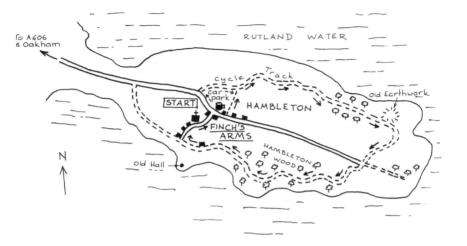

and footpath signpost. The path in question leads down between trees and hedges, through an old sheep pen and down towards the waters' edge across a grassy slope. The cycle track will be reached beyond the next gate, along which you turn right.

The cycle track, which is wide and surfaced with compressed sand and gravel, provides an excellent walking route. It winds a little, and undulates with the contours, but all the while it keeps close to the shore. Along one stretch it passes through a small woodland, along another (at the eastern end) it crosses an old earthwork. Round the corner, returning along the peninsula's south shore, Hambleton Wood is skirted. This was once much larger than it is today, stretching across the pretty Gwash valley. What is now the Peninsula road, which ends abruptly at the eastern end, was formerly the lane to Normanton. The village is now submerged, but its church remains and is visible on the distant shore. It is a fine classical building, today housing a small museum.

Beyond Hambleton Wood the cycle track passes the Old Hall, which stands close to the waters' edge. This was built in 1610 and is the only building to survive the flooding of Middle Hambleton village. Soon after passing this fine manor house leave the cycle track by turning right up the tarmac lane. This leads steeply uphill to Hambleton church and the end of the circular walk. Time should be set aside, however, to explore Hambleton village. There are many old and attractive houses here, notably the church which

Rutland Water.

dates back to Norman times, and Hambleton Hall Hotel with its literary past. When it was a private house, owned by Mrs Astley-Cooper, it played host to Noel Coward.

Places of interest nearby

Around Rutland Water there are many attractions, including a wide range of sporting activities. The *Butterfly and Aquatic Centre*, on the north shore, contains tropical ponds and reptile displays. The town of Oakham has a *Castle* that houses a famous collection of horseshoes, the *Rutland County Museum* and, in Uppingham Road, the *Rutland Farm Park*. The latter has 18 acres of parkland, various farm animals like goats and ponies, and a collection of Victorian farm implements.

19 Greetham
The Wheatsheaf Inn

Dogs allowed in Bar area

The most interesting cottages in the village, and the church itself, stand amongst the lanes north of the main road. Beside Great Lane is an especially curious building, once owned by a Victorian stonemason. It contains fragments of a Gothic window and carvings embedded in its walls.

The Wheatsheaf Inn, which does stand on the main road, occupies an 18th-century building. It has been a tavern since the 1860s and continues to be a friendly and welcoming establishment. Inside, all is traditional with low ceilings, bare stone walls and fireplaces, wooden furniture and various pictures of wildlife and country scenes. There is one main bar, but to the right as you enter is an area housing the pool table, while at the back a large section is set aside as a restaurant. Families are very welcome inside and out. In fine weather many customers sit in the garden by the car park.

Tetley's real ale is served, also Dry Blackthorn cider and numerous wines. But it is the food on offer that especially attracts both locals and travellers – this is exceptionally varied and of high quality. Regular menu items are supplemented by daily specials and there is something for everyone, even vegetarians. Bar snacks include sandwiches, burgers, jacket potatoes, salads and samosas; main meals range from steaks and chicken to pasta bakes and fish dishes; desserts include cakes, ices and puddings with custard. The 'pot' meals and 'skewers' are especially popular.

The Wheatsheaf also offers bed and breakfast facilities, and keeps to normal pub opening times.

Telephone: 01572 812325.

How to get there: Greetham is located on the B668, about a mile west of Stretton and the A1. Oakham lies 6 miles south-west and Stamford is 8 miles south-east. The Wheatsheaf Inn is situated at the eastern end of the village.

Parking: There is a pub car park. Vehicles can also be left in the side streets where space permits, but preferably not along the B668 itself.

Length of the walk: 4 miles. OS map: Landranger 130 Grantham (inn GR 931143).

The Viking Way runs through Greetham. This is a long distance footpath linking Oakham with the Humber Estuary, a distance of 120 miles. North of Greetham, beyond Thistleton, it follows the Leicestershire and Lincolnshire border along a prehistoric trackway known as The Drift. This circular walk begins along the Viking Way heading south from Greetham. At the edge of Exton Park, the route leaves the long distance footpath, to run eastwards to Quinton Lodge, where there is a golf course. The return is made along the valley of North Brook. The trackways followed are clearly marked throughout and the terrain is very easy to cross.

The Walk

Walk west along the B668, past the petrol filling station, and turn left up the footpath signposted as the Viking Way. This will be found almost opposite Great Lane, which is on the north side of the main road. The signpost also informs you that Exton is 2 miles away, although, of course, you will not be going that far. The route is clearly marked. Up some steps and alongside a stone wall, the path proceeds to a stile. Beyond this it runs by a fence, over another

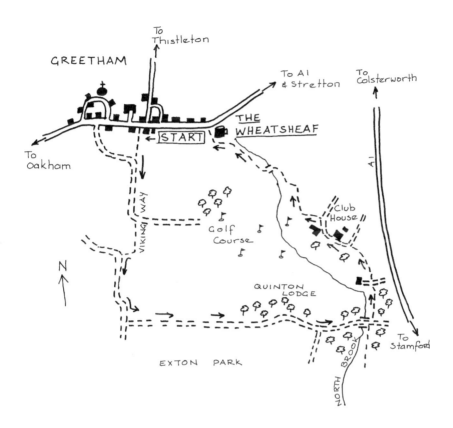

stile and on beside a field used in summer for tents and caravans. Over a cattle-grid it continues as a gravel trackway, dipping down into a shallow valley. Where this gravel track turns left, however, you go straight on along the edge of a large field, keeping the hedgerow to your right. At the far corner a plank bridge and stile lead through to the next field. Turn immediately right, soon to join another gravel trackway, and turn left. A footpath signpost points the way south.

After a short distance, this trackway kinks and meets another trackway, which is on the left. At this point you leave the Viking Way, which continues south. Take the trackway on the left and follow this for more than a mile. Exton Park is now on your right-hand side. A pretty little valley marks its northern edge and the countryside beyond becomes more wooded. In due course the track reaches an area of young trees. Ignoring another track leading off to the right, continue down into a little wooded valley. At the bottom, a footpath signposted to the right is soon followed by another signposted to the left. Follow the latter. A rough flight of steps leads you down under the trees and the path continues on alongside the river. This is a lovely little stretch, and it is hard to believe that the busy A1 is a matter of yards away. Its traffic can be heard but not seen.

Keeping close to the river, which is on the left, continue along some field edges and over several stiles. Cross a tarmac track (which leads to a house) and skirt a grassy hillslope. Cross a gravel track and go over a stile to follow another track towards some modern barns. On the far side of these you reach the golf course club house. Throughout this section, arrow discs mark the route so there should be no trouble finding the way.

The route beyond the club house is equally well signposted. Keeping this building to your left, follow the gravel track that leads between the golf links. At first there is a hedgerow on your left, then later there is one to your right. A stile in the latter hedgerow soon takes you through to the farmland beyond the golf course. Greetham can now be seen ahead. Skirt the edge of the first field and then, over the next stile, aim for the bottom corner. From there the way is clear. Along the valley bottom, by the field edge and a plank bridge, the path follows the river all the way up to the village. Conveniently, you emerge at the back of the Wheatsheaf Inn.

Places of interest nearby

Near Cottesmore (2 miles west) is the *Rutland Railway Museum*, showing steam and diesel locomotives as used for the transport of iron ore in the 19th century. *Wymondham Windmill* (5 miles northwest) is a restored, five-storey tower mill dating from 1814. *Rutland Water*, of course, is only 4 miles away to the south.

20 Clipsham
The Olive Branch Inn

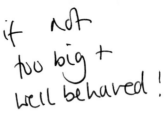

Dogs allowed if not too big + well behaved!

This attractive little village was once famous for its quarries, which lie to the east. The oolitic limestone from these was a much sought after building material and can be found in Burghley House, near Stamford, and in the Houses of Parliament.

The Olive Branch Inn is also made from this stone, and a very handsome building it is too. Inside, all is old and traditional with low beamed ceilings, exposed stone fireplaces and plain walls hung with pictures and brassware. There is one bar counter serving three separate sitting areas, one of these being a lounge, another functioning as a dining room. An annexe is also used for bar snacks. Families are very welcome.

Various real ales are served, the selection often including Hancocks HB, Batemans XB and Ruddles Best. Draught cider may also be on offer, as well as a number of stouts and wines – the brands changing from time to time, as the Olive Branch is a free house. But the quality of the food here never changes, it is always excellent. From toasted sandwiches and salads to steak and kidney pie, trout, chilli con carne and lasagne, the choice should suit everyone. Vegetarian dishes include such items as broccoli and mushroom mornay. Daily specials are written up on a large blackboard in the lounge.

This is a cosy and friendly establishment, popular with locals and tourists alike. It keeps normal pub opening times.

Telephone: 01780 410355.

How to get there: Clipsham is located in the north-east corner of Rutland, 2 miles east of the A1 and 7 miles north of Stamford. The Olive Branch Inn stands in the centre of the village, south of the church.

Parking: There is a pub car park and vehicles can also be left along the lane that leads north to the church. In addition there is a large free car park a mile away, at the entrance to Yew Tree Avenue, which figures in the suggested circular walk.

Length of the walk: 2 miles (3½ mile longer option). OS map: Landranger 130 Grantham (inn GR 969162).

North-east of Clipsham, beyond the privately owned estate of Clipsham Hall, is Clipsham Park Wood which is owned by the Forestry Commission. In this area walkers are welcome and various paths and tracks have been laid out so that country lovers can enjoy the wildlife and scenery. Yew Tree Avenue, which cuts through the middle of this woodland, is justifiably famous and should not be missed. This circular walk takes in Yew Tree Avenue. However, the suggested route should be seen only as a guide, as visitors can stroll at will along the woodland paths. A longer circuit of 3½ miles is possible for those interested in seeing more of the countryside around Clipsham.

The Walk

Those who do not wish to walk from the Olive Branch Inn can drive to the northern end of Yew Tree Avenue and park at the gravel area set aside, next to the entrance lodges. There, amongst the trees, picnic tables are also provided. Those who do walk from the pub should follow the road out of the village, in the direction of Little Bytham and Castle Bytham, and then turn left through the first gate

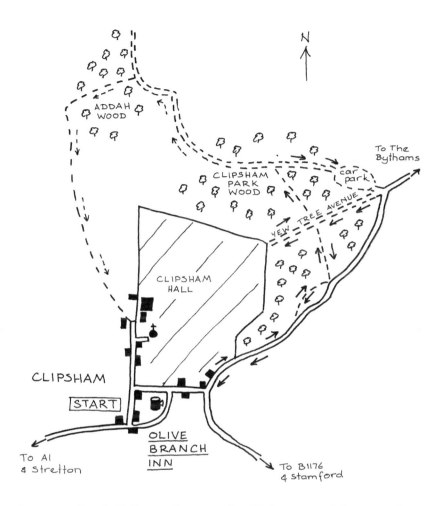

into woodland. Follow a forest path which curves right to reach a wooden bar gateway. From there they turn left along another grassy track. This will bring them to the middle of Yew Tree Avenue.

Now managed by Forest Enterprise, this Avenue once formed the entrance drive to Clipsham Hall. It was planted in the 18th century and consists of 150 yew trees, forming two double rows stretching for ½ mile. But what makes this especially fascinating is the topiary. The yews are all clipped into sugar-loaf shapes, these being topped by other more bizarre creations. There are birds and fish, astronomical symbols and local characters. In relief on the sides of the inner yew trees are inscriptions and other designs, the whole forming a curious and eccentric tapestry of form. Forest Enterprise clips these trees annually each autumn, so their unique patterns are maintained with exemplary precision.

By walking down to the bottom (western) end of the Avenue, you can see the classical façade of Clipsham Hall in the distance. Returning to the middle, a forest glade leads off the northern side. By following this you will reach a main gravel track. By turning right you will eventually reach the eastern end of the Avenue, where stand the entrance lodges, car park and picnic tables. If you are walking back to the Olive Branch Inn you should walk down the Avenue, back to the middle, and then retrace your earlier steps, along the forest paths to the road.

Those intent on a longer walk, to see something of the countryside north of Clipsham village, should follow the gravel track westwards. In due course they will reach Addah Wood. A bridleway through this will take them to the western edge of the trees. From there a clear track heads towards Clipsham church, situated at the end of the lane that leads down to the Olive Branch Inn.

Places of interest nearby

At Tolethorpe Hall (5 miles south-east, near Stamford) is the *Rutland Open Air Theatre* where Shakespearian plays are performed in summer months. *Stamford* itself, of course, should not be missed, it being a fine example of a medieval town. *Burghley House* stands just outside. This is an Elizabethan mansion surrounded by a parkland landscaped by 'Capability' Brown.